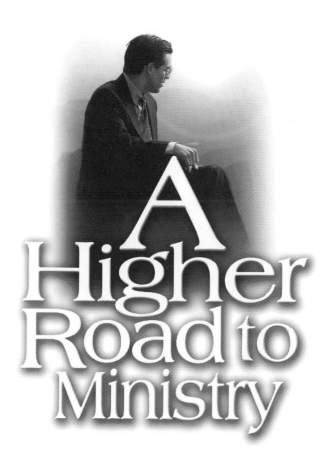

A Higher Road to Ministry

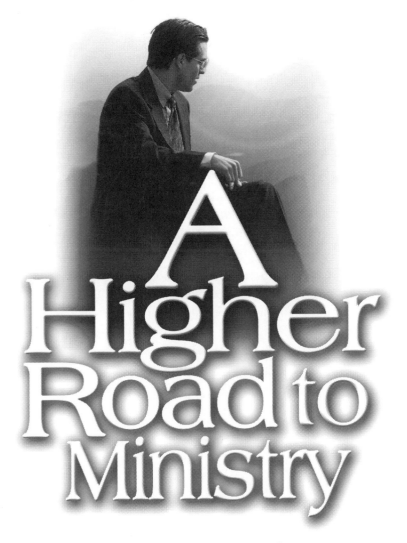

A Higher Road to Ministry

M.G. McLuhan
Foreword by John H. Stoll

Library of Congress Control Card Number: 2001088184
ISBN: 0-87148-049-2
Copyright © 2001 by Pathway Press
Cleveland, Tennessee 37311
All Rights Reserved
Printed in the United States of America

DEDICATION

This book is dedicated to my beloved wife

Merle

a dedicated angel who has stood with me as we labored in Bible colleges, radio ministry, special seminars, foreign missions and pastoral ministry until our retirement on December 31, 1985. A skilled accompanist on the piano, she has helped make my solos a blessing to many.

God has blessed us with three children. Our oldest son, **Dwayne,** is an accomplished choir master who conducts special seminars for others of his profession.

Darlia is the mother of three children. Two of them teach and work at the university where her husband is president, and her youngest daughter is a pastor's wife. Darlia holds a graduate degree in piano and plays for graduate student recitals in addition to her numerous family and university activities.

Our youngest son, **Derryck**, is vice president of a Christian organization providing teaching and special counseling to Christian leadership in the United States and other countries. He has served as a missionary for nearly 20 years in Europe, Russia and Siberia.

Thanks to Merle's Christ-exalting example in our home and around the family altar, our seven grandchildren and five great-grandchildren are all serving God.

TABLE OF CONTENTS

Foreword 9

Introduction 11

Preface 13

1. Being a Man or Woman of God 17
2. Preach the Word 25
3. The Perils of a Holy Calling 33
4. Identifying and Maintaining Goals 47
5. Let God Supply the Miracle 59
6. Escaping the Performance Syndrome 69
7. The Peril of Privilege 77
8. The Peril of Professionalism 83
9. Setting a Guard Over the Mind 91
10. A Christian Work Ethic 105
11. The Futility of Fretfulness 117
12. The Anathema of Avarice 127
13. The Crux of Christian Counseling 135
14. The Terror of Becoming a Castaway 143
15. A Tragic Barter of Basic Christian Vision . . 149
16. The Penalty for Pulpit Perjury 157
17. The Sacredness of Holy Things and Seasons
    165
18. Maintaining Basic Christianity 171
19. Dangers That Lurk on the Alternate Road . . 177

20. Are You Living at Wit's End Corner?. 183
21. Self-Examination, the Supreme Test. 191
22. Dealing With Questions of Holiness and Sin . . . 197
23. Moving Against Disturbing Trends 213
24. Dissidence: Destroyer of Unity and Fellowship
    221
25. A Hard Look at Congregational Autonomy . . 229
26. Fanaticism, Secularism and Faith Interpret
    Tragedy 245
27. Why We Need a Code of Ethics 251
28. Church Staff Ethics 255
29. Disciplined by Grace 261
30. Entertainment in the Sanctuary 267
31. Spiritual Unity: A Timely Awakening 273
32. The Poverty of a Novelty Religion 279
33. The Biblical Demand for Pastoral Constancy . . 285
34. The Final Word: The Grace of God 291

FOREWORD

This Biblical and practical book by Dr. McLuhan is the seminal work of a minister of the gospel who has had a lifetime of service for the Lord. Written in a practical manner, it is carved out of years of service and based on a practical application of Scriptural principles.

Reading the manuscript, I was impressed with the manner in which he discusses principles, and the illustrations from his years as a pastor, missionary and college president. Each avenue of ministry helped weave a fabric of practical admonitions that every pastor and seminary student ought to understand.

Having served the Lord for over 50 years, and having seen the pitfalls and casualties of God's servants, I can only wish that everyone might have had this book to help them avoid the problems they faced over the years.

No young pastor can envision the issues and hazards that lie ahead. This book will make him aware of what he faces and provide him with a Biblical understanding of what to do to keep right with the Lord. I heartily recommend this work. "Keep your heart with all diligence, for out of it spring the issues of life" (Proverbs 4:23).

—John H. Stoll, Th.M., Ph.D.
Executive Director, ASK, Inc.

INTRODUCTION

In *A Higher Road to Ministry*, Dr. M.G. McLuhan shares a lifetime of personal ministry experience that will be valuable for every pastor and aspiring minister in the church today.

Having known the author all of my life as a close associate of my father, Paul H. Walker, and as a trusted partner in ministry at Mount Paran Church of God for 16 years, it is my pleasure to recommend this volume as a significant resource for every person involved in preaching and teaching the gospel.

In his hard-hitting style, he "cuts to the chase" and gives keen insight into the lifestyle of a true minister, the servant of God. This work emphasizes important implications for Scriptural ministry in secular times.

I recommend this enlightening and inspirational book to every person who is interested in being used of the Lord as an "epistle of Christ . . . written . . . by the Spirit of the living God," and "known and read by all men" (see 2 Corinthians 3:2, 3).

—Paul L. Walker, Ph.D.
Chancellor
Church of God Division of Education
Pastor Emeritus
Mount Paran Church of God, Atlanta, Georgia

PREFACE

I was born on a farm in the southwest corner of Saskatchewan, Canada. My parents established a homestead there during the second decade of the 20th century, where on a clear day we could see the foothills of the magnificent Rocky Mountains. Humbly educated but industrious, my father carved a small empire out of the bare prairies and did his best to serve God and family.

My mother was a schoolteacher before she married, and my command of the English language comes from her stern insistence that I learn and practice the "King's English." Our family struggled through the Great Depression. Mother parched wheat to make imitation coffee, and we ordered good used clothes from companies in Toronto and New York. My paternal grandfather lived with us until my 10th year. Every morning he rose with the sun, worked in his garden until breakfast, then read God's Word and led the family in prayer.

In 1928, he slept late one morning, then came out of the bedroom and called my father, who was harnessing the horses for the day's work. Granddad calmly announced, "Today is my last day on earth." He had a dream in which an angel appeared and showed him what eternity with God would be like. Excitedly, he said, "I saw hanging grapes in the gardens of God. The angel said, 'Tomorrow you will come to dwell in this beautiful place.'" My grandfather returned to bed that afternoon. My parents called neighbors, who visited and went home, leaving their best wishes with us. About 9 p.m., Granddad laid his hands on my brother and me and claimed us for God's service. After praying with our parents, he folded his arms across his heart and went quietly into the presence of God.

In the midst of the Depression in 1931, my father was deeply worried. Harvest time was coming, but there was little grain to harvest. While in town to get some machine parts he had ordered, he was delayed by a late-arriving train and had supper at a little Chinese café. As he was putting his repair items in the car, he noticed a man taking a guitar, Bible and hymn books into the town hall. The stranger invited Dad to stay for the meeting, but he replied, "I'm not dressed for church."

"Man looks on the outward appearance, but God looks on the heart," the man, Paul H. Walker, responded. "He thinks your clothes are fine." The stranger was in our community as field representative for the Church of God in Canada. During 55 years in God's service, he founded Northwest Bible College and planted 67 new churches.

Despite his quiet, unassuming manner, Paul Walker's power in the pulpit was legendary. Perched on a three-legged stool, strumming a guitar, he spoke simply to people about Jesus. With Grandfather gone, a powerful influence was missing at our breakfast table, and my father was looking for the God whom Grandfather knew. We attended the meetings, and both of my parents found Christ. In April 1932, my brother and I accepted the Lord. God had come to our home in a real way, family prayers were restored, and Christ became our Lord!

The only relative in Christian ministry was my mother's uncle, Dr. Angus Graham, past moderator of the Presbyterian Church in Canada. He was a man of God, but since he was 2,000 miles away, his ministry did not influence us. We joined the congregation formed from Paul Walker's early meetings.

My brother and I were in the youth group and were encouraged to seek God's will for work in His kingdom. From grade 6, my teachers and friends knew I planned to be a teacher, so they called me "Prof," for "professor." Ministry was not in my plans. But God began speaking to me about what I should do for Him! For the first time I began praying for His direction. The more I prayed, the more urgent the matter became!

At a youth service, Paul Walker emphasized the need for young people to prepare for service in the body of Christ. He asked for testimonies, and I wanted to declare my love for Jesus and acknowledge that He was dealing with me. As the Spirit anointed my testimony, Paul Walker said, "He will one day preach the gospel!" That was blessed confirmation, but a struggle began.

My father had given me 320 acres for my own. So I went to school, worked on the farm and attended a Bible training school at night. One day I sat on my tractor, making laps around the field (what I had always dreamed of doing), when God spoke: "How long will you sit on this tractor when I'm trying to get you to hear My voice?" My father found me with tears making tracks down my face. "You're having a hard time with God's call, aren't you?" I hoped he would say something to ease my inner torment. "Well," he said, "the matter is between you and God, and neither your mother nor I would dare to intrude." At camp meeting that summer, in a moment of surrender, I felt a definite call to Christian ministry!

God gave me a committed Christian bride in 1940—Estella Merle Reesor/McLuhan—my beloved "Merle!" For more than 60 years, God has blessed our family from near poverty, treading a lonely and distant missionary path in the African bush, to associate pastor in a large and prestigious congregation in America. We are deeply thankful that our seven grandchildren and five great-grandchildren are being raised in Christian families.

Pastors sometimes walk in a flower-bedecked landscape. At other times they travel through somber graveyards of heartbreak and failure. Take courage as you begin your pastoral ministry. Your road will not be easy, but it can be long and rewarding. Don't be discouraged by sacrifices you have to make; the rewards you experience from seeing changed lives will be ample spiritual remuneration.

One day, in the land of eternal springtime, God will reward you for your ministry in the presence of His Son, Jesus Christ.

CHAPTER 1

BEING A MAN OR WOMAN OF GOD

*O*f the terms used to describe a servant of Christ, the most desirable is "a man or woman of God." This designation supersedes other descriptive titles such as "a man of the people," "a man of the Word," or "a man of truth." While it provokes an appalling sense of unworthiness, it is undoubtedly the highest tribute to which any Christian leader can aspire. Paul wrote to Timothy, a young pastor at Ephesus:

> Now godliness with contentment is great gain. For we brought nothing into this world, and it is certain we can carry nothing out. And having food and clothing,

with these we shall be content. But those who desire to be rich fall into temptation and a snare, and into many foolish and harmful lusts which drown men in destruction and perdition. For the love of money is a root of all kinds of evil, for which some have strayed from the faith in their greediness, and pierced themselves through with many sorrows.

But you, O man of God, flee these things and pursue righteousness, godliness, faith, love, patience, gentleness. Fight the good fight of faith, lay hold on eternal life, to which you were also called and have confessed the good confession in the presence of many witnesses. I urge you in the sight of God who gives life to all things, and before Christ Jesus who witnessed the good confession before Pontius Pilate, that you keep this commandment without spot, blameless until our Lord Jesus Christ's appearing (1 Timothy 6:6-14).

Pastors of God's sheep, and anyone involved in Christian leadership, should ponder seriously the apostle's instructions in these powerful verses. They spell out the fundamental principles a man or woman of God should model. Pastors are under constant scrutiny by both hurting and healthy Christians who look to them to demonstrate compassion, understanding, righteousness, godliness, faith, love, patience and meekness.

We must ask ourselves, "If I am not a genuine man of God, then how do my people see me? More importantly, how does God see me? We are also carefully observed by non-Christians. What we are when we are not in the pulpit speaks louder than our pulpit utterances.

Instructing God's Shepherds

Look at Paul's detailed instructions to Timothy and to all who feel called to various fields of Christian leadership:

Verse 3. The man of God must watch his words. The spoken word is the basic medium he uses in communicating with people. His speech must be in keeping with the words of Jesus in meaning, truthfulness and doctrinal purity.

Verses 4, 5. Paul warns all pastors called of God that carelessness with words is perilous. Used with any motive other than Christ-centeredness, they cause confusion, wrangling, suspicion and abandonment of fundamental truth.

Verses 6-10. In these five verses Paul speaks generally of the devastating curse of money-lust and the inordinate desire for luxurious living. The man of God must bear in mind that while he can expect to have his material needs provided by his flock, he must not strive for wealth that would place him above the average level of his parishioners.

Obviously, this caution does not apply to the mature Christian leader who has, through years of trial and error, learned the Scriptural principles of tithing and stewardship. A person like this can, indeed, be a positive influence and role model to the younger man and woman of God in regard to matters of money.

Verses 9, 10. Paul points out that those Christian leaders who have succumbed to the *love* of money have destroyed themselves, nullified their impact, and pierced themselves and those who love them with many sorrows.

Verse 11. This verse is key in this whole passage. Paul encourages Timothy to flee the sins and errors mentioned in the preceding verses.

Verses 12-14. This is the confession the true man of God must make before the world and his Christian charges on earth. Believers must pursue righteousness, godliness, faith, love, patience and gentleness. These are the virtues that the heart of a man of God must follow daily.

Whether a young, inexperienced pastor just out of seminary or Bible college or a seasoned servant of God, one must be committed to a lifelong journey in becoming more and more like his Master, Jesus Christ. He must discover for himself what it means to be *out* of the world, yet *in* the world and not *of* the world. He must also realize, however, that with it all, he is obligated *to* the world in his ministry!

I once reviewed this passage with some of my pastoral theology students. One of them remarked, "This passage frightens me greatly. I don't think anyone can live up to it." "You're right," I responded, "if you anticipate achieving it in your own strength."

"Do you think the apostle Paul ever achieved the level of his own instruction?" he asked.

"Why don't you read Philippians 4:13 to the class?" I suggested. The discussion that followed revealed what Paul had discovered: "I can do all things through Christ who strengthens me."

The only way to live up to Paul's injunction is to have an intimate relationship with the Lord. In this way, one can obtain the mind of Christ and gain essential spiritual strength and stature.

Inspired by this discovery, one young man uttered a statement that has stayed with me all these years: "God helping me I will supply the man, but God will have to supply the grace and spiritual strength if I am ever to be a man of God!" It is an impossible objective to set unless one learns just what it means to walk in the power and enablement of the Holy Spirit!

Committing to Ministry

A born-again believer called into Christian leadership will never be a man or woman of God without a complete commitment to the call and to the God who called them! Becoming a servant of God is accomplished over a lifetime. It comes from an extended period of growing in God's grace. What we know, be it ever so profound, does not help us to reach the Christlike level we profess if we have not reached it in fact!

Claiming to be something does not make it a fact. Those who know us best will be the first to recognize if we are truly men and women of God! And to attempt to reach this New Testament objective does not rob us of our humanity. I have known men and women who, without question, have reached this spiritual stature. I think of Dr. Billy Graham, whose life and ministry have proven beyond doubt that he is a genuine man of God. His impact on struggling humanity has proved it!

Billy Graham is not alone. Hundreds more have reached this most noble level of servanthood. The burning question that haunts those trying to become men and women of God in their own strength is, "Just whose man or woman are you?" One may do quite well in deceiving his or her human flock for a while. Sooner or later, however, what a person really is will come through his pretensions, and the people will see the hypocrisy.

Bear in mind that for you or me to be a man or woman of God doesn't mean we have reached perfection. It does mean, however, that we are on the road to that state. We will enjoy perfection in its completeness only in the presence of our Lord Himself in eternity.

Years ago my teacher/mentor advised our seminary class that every pastor should read Paul's first letter to Timothy at least once a month. Over the years this has proven to be wonderful counsel. The letter, for Timothy and for all of God's shepherds, instructs in family living, wise stewardship, the mystery of godliness, how children should behave, and even the value of physical exercise. In chapter 4, Paul emphasizes God's Word:

Give attention to reading, to exhortation, to doctrine. . . . Meditate on these things; give yourself entirely to them, that your progress may be evident to all. Take heed to yourself and to the doctrine. Continue in them, for in doing this you will save both yourself and those who hear you (vv. 13, 15, 16).

This advice is for all who wish to have a meaningful and contemporary message. Every true man or woman of God must guard against pride and an exaggerated sense of self-importance. We as God-called individuals must realize that our position is in many ways more critical than that of the people we serve. We are constantly under a social and spiritual microscope. For others to consider us as shepherds of God, we must walk with Him in our earthly pilgrimage.

Modeling Christ's Behavior

Both the leader and his family must model an appropriate lifestyle. Otherwise, they unwittingly become the justification for careless, godless living by those looking to excuse their own improper conduct. God's servants must not strive for this level of achievement for their own glory. Rather, they must reveal Christ to searching humanity.

Nothing wounds the body of Christ more than servants of God who fall morally, spiritually and socially. A godless world looks on with gleeful satisfaction when they see God's leaders exposed because of lust, greed, pride or carnality. Our task is to share the gospel of reconciliation and restoration. We must continually monitor ourselves in light of the effect our lives have on others.

Builder or Wrecker

I watched them tearing a building down,
A gang of men in a busy town.
With a ho-heave-ho and a lusty yell,
They swung the beams and the sidewalls fell.

I asked the foreman, "Are these men skilled,
The kind you'd hire were you to build?"
He laughed and said, "Why, no indeed!
Just common laborers are all I need.
They can easily wreck in a day or two
What builders have taken years to do."

And I thought to myself as I went my way:
"What part in the game of life do I play?
Am I a builder who works with care,
Making the world better because I was there?
Am I shaping my deed to a well-made play,
Patiently doing my best each day?

Or am I a wrecker who walks the town,
Content with the labor of tearing down?"
– Unknown

Do others see you as a wrecker or as a builder?

CHAPTER 2

PREACH THE WORD

*I*n the apostle Paul's last epistle, his second letter to Timothy, he gave his young pastor-friend and son in the faith this stern charge: "Preach the word! Be ready in season and out of season. Convince, rebuke, exhort, with all long-suffering and teaching" (2 Timothy 4:2). Paul then prophesied that a time would come when some would not endure sound doctrine, but would turn away their ears from the truth and listen to fables or false teachings (vv. 3, 4).

In the new century, Christian leaders and Bible-loving Christians of all denominations are expressing concern that genuine Bible preaching, as such, is declining in favor of popular themes, political considerations and other matters of contemporary interest. Learned Bible teachers are not in demand by local churches. Music groups, drama teams, special soloists and skilled musicians are being used effectively. They attract large crowds, and there is nothing wrong with that. But *crowd building* is not always *soulwinning* or *disciple making!*

A prime reason for the lack of lay involvement in evangelism is the common error that arises from translating Paul's original words. The Greek word he used for "preach" is *keruxon,* which means "to proclaim." Paul referred to public speaking when he wrote this passage to Timothy, and the Great Commission speaks of disciple making!

> Go therefore and make disciples of all the nations, baptizing them in the name of the Father and of the Son and of the Holy Spirit, teaching them to observe all things that I have commanded you; and lo, I am with you always, even to the end of the age (Matthew 28:19, 20).

The body of Christ is charged with the responsibility of equipping every believer to proclaim the gospel in the most effective way possible. Our Lord commanded us to teach the basic principles of the gospel, and this cannot be done without the Bible, which is the center of the teaching process. Disciple making begins with preaching, but it also calls for teaching, modeling and instructions in living, speaking, thinking and understanding what the Christian life is all about. This focuses on the absolute necessity of studying, preaching and teaching the great truths of the Bible!

> For the Word of God is living and operative and sharper beyond every two-edged sword, and passing through as far as division of soul and spirit, of joints and marrow, and able to judge the thoughts and intentions of the heart (Hebrews 4:12, *free translation*).

I marvel at some of my ministerial colleagues who invent catchy titles for their sermons and Biblical lectures. They seem to think that this makes the message more palatable to the people. My ministry has proven to me, however, that a diligent study of the Scriptures always supplies me with more preaching material than I can use! The spiritually convicting power of our messages will be in direct proportion to how genuine they are in Scriptural content.

The power of the Holy Spirit in the preaching of the Word makes our message powerful and convicting. Hebrews emphasizes with clarity that the Word of God is alive. Contrary to the beliefs of some, the Bible is not a dead form of ancient literature. It remains constantly fresh and applicable to our lives, our problems and our searching questions. The Bible is the written form of God's words.

1. God's Word is currently operative. No problem can occur in our lives the Word of God cannot apply (and for which it cannot furnish) answers. Its uplifting instructions are always current. It always speak to the immediate present. It always addresses our needs!

2. God's Word is penetrating, convicting and instructive. Its identification of evil and disobedience is sharp, clear and totally impartial. The great and the small, the weak and the strong stand equal before its heart-searching power.

3. God's Word reveals the human spirit. The Word of God exposes those things we feel in our very bones (joints and marrow), even if we haven't revealed them to another living soul!

4. God's Word discerns thoughts and hidden intentions. As preachers of the gospel we must never feel that the conviction and conversion of those who have sinned is the result of our persuasiveness. When we preach the Word of God under the inspiration of the Holy Spirit, we will observe the power of that Word doing its wonderful work. It has nothing to do with cleverness or impressive delivery.

Paul instructed Timothy to preach the Word! The same is true of lay witnessing or personal soulwinning. When we accurately quote God's Word, it convicts of sin and evil, and instructs in righteousness. When we preach the Word in modern terms but with interpretative accuracy, we are always contemporary and effective in ministry!

God's Word is our only authority for defining His will. We must never get the idea that God's Word is outdated or that modern society has moved into some state not addressed in the Word of God! For at least 3,000 years, Holy Scriptures have been revered and respected by God's people. Psalm 119, the longest chapter in the Bible, is dedicated to God's ancient revelation of Himself.

The awe-inspiring Scriptures have been looked on with holy fear, and it began soon after the dawn of inspired writing. A written copy of His revealed will to humanity is the most sacred document in our possession. The Scriptures are the most comprehensive record we have of God's dealings with humanity. They reach through the centuries to reveal the vagaries of man's behavior on earth. They reveal his search for and discovery of Deity. Regardless of the difficulty we are passing through, the Word of God has the answers!

"Be eager to present yourself approved to God, an unashamed workman, cutting straight the Word of truth" (2 Timothy 2:15, *literal translation*). The Greek for "cutting straight" is *orthotomounta*, an accusative singular masculine participle, the present tense of *orthotomeo* which means "to cut straight, to set forth truthfully, or to define without perversion or distortion." All who preach and teach God's Word must do so without bias or distortion. To make it say what it doesn't say, whether deliberately or ignorantly, is inexcusable in a day of advanced research and technology.

Revelation 22:18, 19 warns that if we take from or add to the Revelation, our names will be taken from the Book of Life and we'll suffer the plagues identified there! We will too if we distort or neglect *any* of God's Word! Every Christian should be able to trust his pastor or teacher's public interpretation of the Bible implicitly. People put a sacred trust in us when they consider us their spiritual guides and instructors. God's Word is the basic source of divinely inspired revelation to His children.

Every moment we spend in dedicated and scholarly study of Holy Scriptures will be rewarded in His sanctuary and classroom! A Christian preacher who avoids studying and preaching the Word, or downplays its importance as a divine revelation from God, should realize that he or she is senselessly detracting from the only accepted source of instructive authority and pastoral leadership.

Many struggle to find the way without knowing what God's Word says. The Word is "a lamp to my feet and a light to my path" (Psalm 119:105). In an era with no definitives or absolutes, to whose voice are we to listen? The cacophony that screams a thousand untested instructions to us? Or the ageless Word of God speaking in definite terms? We who preach the gospel are God's mouthpieces. Do we proclaim the words of His guidance? Or are we confusing an already confounded world, compounding the spiritual and moral perplexity of a groping generation? We must simply *preach the Word!*

As messengers of God's truth, we cannot water down the Word for Biblically-incorrect viewpoints. We don't need the influence or the money of those who support heretical concepts. Gentle confrontation often corrects those who water down the Word; they must know that there can be no compromise with God's Word. We are better off without the incorrigible and their heresy. Christian love dwells only in tents of transparent truth!

Renowned men of God—Dr. Billy Graham, Dr. James Dobson, Dr. Charles Stanley, Dr. Charles Swindoll and Dr. Robert Schuller—take the pure, unadulterated Word of God all across the United States and the world. Others who are not so well known labor diligently alongside them. Without exception, the primary, distinguishing feature of these ministries is their unquestioned fidelity to God's eternal Word. We must take a lesson from their excellent work and try to emulate it in our local churches. What I am writing primarily to pastors, I say to every Christian, "Let us *all* get back to the plain and simple preaching and teaching of the Bible."

A common burden borne by God's leaders and pastors is frequently expressed, "Let the preacher do it. This is what God called him to do and it is why we are paying his salary." This attitude disparages and disrespects the pastor. It is an excuse to avoid the New Testament position that the "proclaiming" aspect of the gospel is *not* just the job of the preacher or the evangelist. It is just as much the God-given task of the uninformed "squawker" who criticizes his spiritual shepherd but never opens his mouth in witness to sinful humanity.

The duty of "proclaiming" includes the parental

responsibility of seeing that our children are clearly and effectively taught the truths of God's Word. This must begin as soon as the child is old enough to attend a Sunday school class. Let us remember that without God's Word, we have no spiritual authority before God and in the eyes of our people. God's Word is God's words to us! A Christian congregation should be a miniature Bible institute. This applies to every age group in the congregation, and can only be accomplished by making God's Word the living text of faith, practice, hope and instruction!

The truths we preach, the lives we live, the character we demonstrate, the spirit we manifest, and the warmth we allow to flow from our hearts must be based on God's simple and holy truths and His absolute gentle holiness. Proclaim His Word with your lips, your hands, your attitude and with supernatural love.

His Word is the Magna Carta of spiritual liberty; proclaim it every way you can. *Preach the Word* first and foremost, and other responsibilities of your ministry will fall in line.

CHAPTER 3

THE PERILS OF A HOLY CALLING

God calls each and every one of His children to specific service in the Kingdom. In the early days of my ministry, both in teaching and preaching, I encouraged students and church members to diligently seek to discover for themselves the work God had called them to perform. I had not been in Christian ministry long, however, until God brought to my attention the fact that our call to a specialized ministry is secondary to our call to be saints! Paul makes this point clear:

> To all who are in Rome, beloved of God, called to be saints (Romans 1:7).

> To the church of God which is at Corinth, to those who are sanctified in Christ Jesus, called to be saints, with all who in every place call on the name of Jesus Christ our Lord, both theirs and ours (1 Corinthians 1:2).
>
> But as God has distributed to each one, as the Lord has called each one, so let him walk. And so I ordain in all the churches (1 Corinthians 7:17).

Until we recognize our call to sainthood to be a "holy" call, we cannot seek, Biblically, any other kind of personal call to ministry in Christ's body!

During those early years, I encountered much frustration, seeking to know the *will* of God instead of the *heart* of God. The Holy Spirit was dealing with me to deepen my walk in holiness—in thought, disposition, motive and will. Instead of listening, I was begging in tears for God to identify my ministerial call more clearly.

After much tarrying and praying, God finally got across to me that He wanted my heart and inner spirit, then He could use my head, my mouth and my hands! God wants us to understand that before we can demonstrate His power, we must first demonstrate His character and His holiness. Before a lifetime calling is revealed to us, we must permit Christ to be formed within us! "My little children, for whom I labor in birth again until Christ is formed in you" (Galatians 4:19).

The first step that God's called servants must take toward measuring up to a holy call is the achievement of holy thinking. In Romans 12:2, Paul wrote, "And do not be conformed to this world, but be transformed by the renewing of your mind, that you may prove what is that good and acceptable and perfect will of God." We who sense God's call must take personal responsibility for the quality of our thinking.

In a world of X-rated movies, sleazy pornography, verbal blasphemy and risqué jokes, this is not easy. The conquest of our depraved mind is the Holy Spirit's first and greatest task. Proverbs 23:7 declares, "For as he thinks in his heart, so is he." A factor that makes it more difficult is the prevalent notion that we can take a few breaks now and then. No one knows what is going on in our heads, so we take mental excursions into the slime pits of imagination. Then we drag our minds out of the mire, secretly shake off the filth and try to resume our mental concentration on purer thoughts.

The problem is that the footprints made during unholy mental excursions remain in the pathways of our mind! They pop up at unguarded moments as we are attempting to focus on God. They mar the mental landscape with their stinking influence! In counseling I have interviewed Christians, even a few preachers, who described this mental slavery that cursed their thinking with ungodliness in the midst of reading their Bible or preparing a sermon. Every man and woman of God must come to the place where at the very first moment of mental laxity, they have the spiritual alertness to rebuke Satan and the evil thought itself. They must force their minds to return to holy ground. We must not say that this is impossible. Countless thousands of God's people have proven to themselves that by the grace of God and the help of the Holy Spirit they could, and did, do it!

Only insidious hypocrisy permits our minds to run willy-nilly wherever Satan leads, and then step to the pulpit and express the holy utterances we developed in moments when we *were* mentally in step with God! A recognition of the holiness of our calling causes us to seek the face of God in our pilgrimage toward Christ-centered thinking. It is possible to conquer our wandering imaginations. The source of holy words and truths are holy thoughts! "As He who called you is holy, you also be holy in all your conduct, because it is written, 'Be holy, for I am holy'" (1 Peter 1:15, 16).

Since the manifestation of genuine mental and spiritual transformation is our most basic God-given assignment, it must be uppermost in whatever service or ministry He gives us to perform. Paul's own testimony bears this out:

> But when it pleased God, who separated me from my mother's womb and called me through His grace, to reveal His Son in me, that I might preach Him among the Gentiles, I did not immediately confer with flesh and blood (Galatians 1:15, 16).

When we recognize that our first calling is to be saints who reveal Christ's holiness in compassion, gentleness, love, grace and forgiveness, God brings our ministry calling into focus. Those who are recognized as great servants in Christian history were first identified as Christlike saints. Their Christlikeness and gentleness of character rather than their specific expertise caused them to be revered! The spirit and heart behind our Christian service shines through. Expertise is soon forgotten, but integrity and holy character are eternal! What dangers imperil our sacred call to holiness?

1. The supernatural can become commonplace and holiness can cease to be an issue. What causes holiness to cease to be an issue? A familiarity which replaces the sense of sacredness. When a pastor officiates at his first Communion or Eucharist, his feelings of awe and wonder prompt him to perform the ritual with dignity and holiness. He prays earnestly that he will move the hearts and minds of his communicants with a sense of the holiness of the sacrament. As time goes by, his sense of the sacred is dimmed because he has learned to perform the ritual without an awareness of God and the meaning of the service. He has to reclaim his dependence on God and the sacredness of the memorial he performs.

2. The tedium of repetition can rob us of the miracle of faith. Ephesians 2:8 reminds us that faith is a miraculous gift of God: "For by grace you have been saved through faith, and that not of yourselves; it is the gift of God." When my first convert to Christ rose from his knees after repentance and prayer, he glowingly described his newfound faith with smiles and tears. My joy knew no bounds. I was aware of his previous life, and his conversion was truly a trophy of grace. I excitedly reported his experience to others who were not present.

As time went on and I became the associate pastor of a large church, I caught myself drifting into an indifferent response to the miracle of the new birth. Under the preaching of a great pastor, many people were finding Christ as Savior in every service, but the wonder of regenerative transformation was becoming lost to my heart. The majesty of the redemptive work of the Holy Spirit was falling victim to the humdrum of repetition. I no longer rejoiced with God's angels over every soul that entered the Kingdom and found eternal life.

One Sunday evening, after many had responded to the pastoral call to come to Christ, I entered the prayer room and within a few moments a young woman in tears raised her hands and began to praise God loudly and to sing. At first I was somewhat irked by her noisy behavior. I went to her side to speak to her. When she saw me she seized my arm and exclaimed, "Pastor, I have just found Christ! I have just been redeemed by His blood!"

That was the shock I needed! The holy glory of it all came back to my heart in a flash, along with my own memories of the night I had found Christ many years before. I begged God to forgive me for my insensitivity, and to restore to me the sense of wonder and glory of His mighty acts.

3. Relationships can become blurred when the demands of people are more important than the commands of God. God's servants who find themselves in a growing pastorate must keep their ears attuned to two distinctly different voices. The twin challenges of hearing the voice of God while listening to a growing congregation and the confused world of the unregenerate we serve make our service more difficult. A person in the ministry without an express call from God must find out whose call he or she has heard! I have spent years training some of the finest and most dedicated people—young and not-so-young—that I was ever privileged to know. I watched them with great interest after they left the training institution.

In the final days of their training, the reality of a divine call became evident as I spoke and prayed with them. With fear and trembling they launched into the unfamiliar field of pastoring their first small congregation—following what they deeply felt was a holy call from God himself! As the years passed, I visited some and discovered that they had gone much deeper in their relationship with God than they had when they left college. They were walking with God, listening intently to His Holy Spirit, and leading their flock along a path that was sometimes tough, but always victorious!

Others were listening only to the whims and wishes of people, and struggling with tasks larger than they could handle. With the former, the holiness and excitement of Christian faith was still bright and real. With the latter, the task was difficult and sometimes nearly hopeless in their eyes. When our tasks as shepherds of a human flock become overwhelming, we must determine whether we are still walking with the Good Shepherd who called us, or whether we are simply keeping step with our sheep!

I do not imply that pastors should ignore the voice of the people. But we must walk so obviously with God that they trust us as God's messengers. If they themselves have to hear God's voice for the congregation, the pastor's true shepherdship over them will be short-lived! When God's call to leadership is a true conviction in the heart of a pastor, his people will sense the holiness and profundity of his shepherdship, and will follow without fear or undue criticism.

4. Burnout can occur and we can lose His power, will and partnership because of self-centeredness. When our holy calling from God becomes so blurred that we feel an undue sense of importance, we need to remember that God the Father, Jesus Christ the Lord, and the Holy Spirit are still ranked far ahead of us. If we habitually speak with God about our tasks and our people, we will have confidence in our own leadership and people will be happy to follow us and provide for us. The holiness of our calling will cause us to be responsible shepherds. We will develop the spiritual skills to lead people into the presence of God!

Many pastors experience burnout because they have taken too much responsibility. They have come to look upon themselves as sole directors of everything that goes on in the parish. They forget that they are to be laborers *together* with others as well as with God!

5. We can excuse our own frailties and failures by pointing to imagined incompetence in those God sends to help us. I once worked with a capable man who for some time became rather downcast and somber. I asked his wife, "What is bothering your husband these days?" "Oh," she said, "he thinks the people on his staff aren't up to scratch in their work, and he doesn't know where to find better helpers." The truth was that his staff would compare favorably with any other staff. They weren't whiz-bang dynamos that he apparently wanted, but they stacked up well.

An hourglass on my desk bears the slogan, "A man is never a failure until he starts blaming someone else for his mistakes!" Bear in mind that we are all human.Those who dream of superhuman helpers will not find them.They are probably pastoring their own churches and are unhappy with their assistants! When we arrive at the top of our own self-constructed ladder, we need to ask God to flash our limitations on the screen of our memories.

6. We are tempted to replace and/or imitate the supernatural works of God and His Holy Spirit. When the church is winning souls to Christ on a regular basis, it is not wrong to develop exciting and impressive programs that bring in the crowds to hear the gospel in word and drama. A common error of some Christian leaders, however, is to refer to such extravaganzas as "the power of God."

Years ago, several popular televangelists were holding large campaigns. On a trip to Western Canada, we stopped at a little church where we used to worship. As we drove up, I noticed that the pastor had loaded his car with people and luggage, and was getting ready to drive off. I asked where he was going, and with a rather mystical air he replied, "Oh, Pastor McLuhan, we are going to hear the great healer!"

I looked at him for a moment and said, "Well, He stands at the right hand of the throne of God, and I do not think you are going to get there in that contraption!" This form of leadership adulation is nothing short of subtle paganism in a pseudo-Christian setting! No human, even the best preacher who ever trod the earth, should be referred to as the "great healer"! We know that God heals in answer to prayer, but He alone is the Great Healer!

When we call ourselves by titles that belong only to God, and when we begin to imitate His supernatural powers, we are in deep trouble! This signals that we have lost our sense of the majesty of God.

Those who degenerate spiritually to the level of self-declared deity have lost the sense of a holy calling and are nothing short of deceivers!

7. We can lose our sense of a holy calling and be program-directed rather than Spirit-directed. There is nothing wrong with setting up a program for a worthwhile presentation in the house of God. But when the congregation and pastoral staff are controlled by schedules and programs, where does the leadership of the Holy Spirit come in? I have known of, and have been involved in, church programs so intense and detailed that the Holy Spirit was never a consideration in the entire scenario. Participants were actually prisoners of the program! Its detailed presentation was all-consuming, and even the usual prayers were shortened for the sake of it.

On the other hand, I have seen programs that were, from the very first note, Christ-exalting and spiritually moving for everyone present. In the first instance, the presentation was the controlling factor; in the other, the holiness of God and the leading of His Spirit were evident, for the emphasis was the exaltation and worship of the Lord Jesus!

8. We can gradually drift toward a social rather than a spiritual emphasis in our worship. This is elusive because it happens gradually. Unless we are perceptive, it takes place before we are aware of it. We must be people-centered with deliberate efforts to increase attendance at our services. However, when we are successful in this endeavor, we can lose the spiritual tone of truly Christ-centered worship. Our people are human, and they enjoy a relaxed social environment just as we do. If we are alert to their needs, we will provide time to socialize as well as to worship.

The problem is that it takes less effort and concentration to provide a social climate than it does to maintain an atmosphere of genuine worship. We soon discover that it's easier to make pleasant and amusing remarks than it is to preach Biblical truths that are not always pleasant to our listeners. We don't have to spend many minutes preparing a lighthearted sermon, but it takes study to prepare a truly Biblical message!

The social sermon contains none of the elements of spiritual truth that cause people to repent of sin and seek the face of God! Generally, the idea of mental and spiritual discipline is repugnant to many church attendees. People do not like to have their mental cages rattled by Biblically based truths that call for radical moral, mental or ethical change.

The truly God-called shepherd of people will realize, however, that his holy task is to challenge parishioners to "lay aside every weight, and the sin which so easily ensnares us, and let us run with endurance the race that is set before us" (Hebrews 12:1).

9. We can use the wrong criteria in choosing our pastoral staff and leaders. The leadership of a 21st-century congregation must indeed be multi-talented and quite complex in its makeup. When choosing a pastoral staff, we ask for problems when we place more emphasis on sharp personalities, high-powered natural giftings, cold technical expertise, educational accomplishments or even wealthy connections, rather than genuine spiritual qualifications.

I remember a qualified but spiritually un-involved sound-control technician who botched many fabulous musical and preaching master-pieces by his carelessness. Truly Christ-centered staff members can be found. The pastor's first consideration must be the leader's spiritual experience with God and his or her commitment to the sacredness of the task of winning and discipling the souls of humankind! Pastoral staff members who are lackadaisical about staff prayer sessions or weak in ministering to hurting and broken people should never be chosen!

I have observed worship leaders who could stir the emotions of a crowd to a fanatical fervor, but walked out of the service as soon as the pastor be-gan to preach the Word! The awesome responsibility involved in leading God's people in worship in His house had apparently never occurred to them. That kind of staff member is an insult to the sacredness of any worship service where God Almighty and His Son, Jesus Christ, are being exalted.

Choosing the wrong pastoral assistants can be

a death knell to the genuine spiritual leadership in a congregation. Make your selections only after diligently seeking the help of the Holy Spirit in the heartfelt fear of God. Committed study and training are important, but there is no substitute for God's call upon leaders. A calling adds a sacred aura to the person's training and education. The called have a focus on the minds and spirits of people on a level far above that of the secular world.

In our service to God and to humanity, we must never lose the sense of the holiness of our mission! We do this only by maintaining a personal relationship with Jesus Christ our Lord!

CHAPTER 4

IDENTIFYING AND MAINTAINING GOALS

*T*his book is dedicated to young men and women who feel the call of God to take up the pastoral ministry. After serving the Lord more than 60 years as a Bible College lecturer and college president, a foreign missionary, a teacher in camp meetings and other conferences, and as the associate pastor in a large and growing church, I have a message for the young pastor!

I share some advice that applies to every generation: If there is to be steady progress in your ministry, it is imperative to set achievable goals. A life without a plan is doomed to failure! Unforeseen circumstances will arise on an almost daily basis, regardless of how high or how moderate your goals may be. These are guidelines:

1. Decide what course to take.
2. Stick with that concept and vision, regardless of the difficulties.
3. Be resilient enough to make changes without losing your focus.

These salient facts were powerfully reinforced in my own experience. My final assignment prior to retirement was associate pastor to a highly successful and capable man of God. His practice was to outline goals he felt God had set for him and the congregation. In the 16 years I served, he never deviated one time from them! We always knew where we were going as a church, and our goals did not change before we reached them!

If the man of God isn't sure where he is going, his congregation will drift spiritually just as he drifts. As shepherds, we must know where we wish to lead our human sheep and how to find sustenance. A church not growing in spiritual experiences is being led by a transient wanderer. Pastors can and must set goals for the future.

No two ministers have the same gifts, abilities, characteristics, or even the same specific calling. Our instructors and other senior men of God who know us intimately can give invaluable assistance in setting realistic goals for ourselves. Paul said: "For I say, through the grace given to me, to everyone who is among you, not to think of himself more highly than he ought to think, but to think soberly as God has dealt to each one a measure of faith" (Romans 12:3). One of my great Bible teachers gave his students a rule for progress in working for Christ:

Start slow, aim low; Rise higher, strike fire. And have enough good sense to stop in the middle of the storm!

"Better to aim low and hit the woodpile than to aim too high and hit nothing!" he explained. Every budding young pastor must strive to follow these rules:

Overestimating Your Abilities

It is better to accept a humble assignment and accomplish it, than to accept a task greater than your abilities and fail dismally. It is better to be promoted by your peers and your seniors for having proved your ability to handle a tough job, than to be seen as one who has overshot his calling!

Honest With Your Own Estimation

If you are married, it is likely your wife can help you genuinely assess your true capabilities and gifts. Dr. James Bruce once gave me some wise counsel. He told me to find an experienced mentor who had been in ministry for some time. He suggested that the mentor should not be from my own denomination, because a secret may be too good to keep.

I found an experienced pastor, Dr. Bear, who pastored a successful Baptist congregation and was a devoted Christian. Young and inexperienced, I needed a mentor like Dr. Bear. I still remember most of the pastoral lessons he taught me. Dr. Bruce's advice had guided me to become the right kind of man. Dr. Bear showed the right kind of love and understanding for a fledgling pastor. His honesty helped me to be honest with myself.

Discovering Your Own Giftings

Having then gifts differing according to the grace that is given to us, let us use them: if prophecy, let us prophesy in proportion to our faith; or ministry, let us use it in our ministering; he who teaches, in teaching; he who exhorts, in exhortation; he who gives, with liberality; he who leads, with diligence; he who shows mercy, with cheerfulness (Romans 12:6-8).

Paul's reference to prophecy referred to proclaiming the gospel. The Greek word for "prophecy" seldom meant prediction, but rather proclamation. The word *ministering* had to do with caring for the needs of God's people.

Overselling Yourself to Others

Know the difference between unrealistic dreams and stark reality. Better to be timid about taking assignments you are not sure of than to take them and not be able to handle them. I served on a Ministerial Examining Committee when a young man declared that he had a powerful and divine call. His former instructors' assessment was that we might find him overaggressive and opinionated.

We asked him, "What would you do if by some unusual circumstance you were asked to pastor a church with 500 members?" He replied, "Oh, I might find it challenging at first, but I think I could handle a charge like that!" Later, he accepted a much smaller congregation; but, unfortunately, even on that level he had oversold himself.

Be happy with a humble beginning, and do your best as though you have a large congregation. Pastors who developed large churches are those who minister to a small church as though it is large, giving all they have in dedication and inspiration.

Time Alone With God

The first goal that anyone preparing for Christian ministry must set is that of time spent in spiritual preparation and in meditation on God and prayer. In a book on pastoral theology, John Henry Jowett remarked that if a minister wasn't in his study in prayer and meditation when he heard the footfalls of his parishioners trudging to their labors early in the morning, that preacher needed to examine his commitment to the ministry and to his people.

Time for prayer and the study of Holy Scripture is the most crucial item on a minister's schedule! Many vital things call for intercession and compassionate personal contact: parishioners, our relationship with the needy in the community, the ill in the congregation, and dozens of other matters.

Time to Communicate

Successful pastors are "people" persons. As a shepherd of souls, you must be warm and approachable. Be available during the regular services for at least a few minutes to share greetings and words of concern with individual members of the flock. Learn to be a pleasant conversationalist—a more difficult task than it once was because television and computer habits have robbed thousands of normal communicative skills. The pastor must be a personable, alert communicator—on a one-on-one basis as well as in the pulpit.

Pastoral counseling is an important focus. A communications goal is to allot space during the week to meet individually with people in genuine Christian counseling. A word of caution: It is imperative to avoid strict privacy in counseling situations. The counseling area should be accessible to and easily monitored by passers-by or casual observers. Yet, it should be out of earshot and at a distance to maintain privacy. We live in a world of slack morals. The counseling pastor must guard against the possibility of an accusation of sexual involvement with his or her counselees.

Practice Personal Contacts

Hospital visits, ministry to shut-ins, urgent family emergencies and other crisis situations require the pastor to be deeply involved and on call by broken and hurting people. While a visitation minister is essential in every large congregation, the face of the pastor in a life-or-death situation is definitely called for.

One of the most effective ministries in the great congregation where I served was our method of dealing with urgent crises. As our congregation grew, the senior pastor told us that if any on the pastoral staff received an urgent call, we were to attend to the crisis immediately and personally. He reminded us that families in our congregation looked on specific men on the staff as being their personal pastor; and that at any hour, day or night, we would receive calls.

My telephone rang at 2:00 one morning. An elder with whom I worked closely on an important church project lay in the hospital with a serious heart attack. His wife called me, and I quickly dressed and drove to the hospital. Members of his family were already there, and when I walked into his room it was as though I was a visiting angel! The elder whispered, "Pastor, I knew you would come. I've seen your love for God's people." What joy we shared when he narrowly survived that attack and recovered almost completely.

I had never realized my prayers were important to that family! The ministry of a hospital-visiting pastor reached the elder during his illness and I called him a number of times on the telephone. For me, it was one of those sacred moments that makes pastoral ministry so rewarding. Compassionate, personal ministry must be a major goal.

Demonstrating a Passion for Souls

If we never weep for and with our human sheep in their trials and struggles, we need never expect to enjoy the spiritual luxury of rejoicing with them! A man so moved that he will weep for others has a particular majesty about him. General Norman Schwarzkopf was asked during the Desert Storm military action: "I understand you often weep with and for your men. Is this true?"

When he said that he did, he was asked, "How does a man who plays such a powerful role in the military find it in himself to weep?" General Schwarzkopf replied that only a leader who cared enough to weep for his men could be a truly compassionate, brave and qualified officer!

Compassion is the ability to feel with those who are wounded and hurting. "Soul passion" weeps for another who is out of touch with God and humanity. When people see a pastor's eyes wet with tears for hurting and straying people, they know that the pastor has a divine soul passion. Just as "Jesus wept," so must we—often (see John 11:35).

Sensitive to the Leading of the Holy Spirit

Learn the difference between a change of mind and the leading of the Holy Spirit. One may plan to preach a specific sermon, but on entering the sanctuary feel impressed to speak on a different theme. This kind of Spirit leading has led me and many of my pastor-friends to powerfully effective preaching changes. In the church I last served, my son-in-law and I were seated on the platform before the senior pastor entered one evening. We felt an unusual sense of God's presence, and he said, "I have a strong feeling that the pastor will not speak on the theme announced in the bulletin." I told him I had the same feeling.

We were deeply moved when the senior pastor stepped into the pulpit and told the congregation, "Friends, I hope you understand that it is my prerogative to change my sermon if I feel led to do so by the Holy Spirit." The message he preached that night without a note was powerful in its spontaneity. When he concluded, nearly everyone, including the staff, was on their knees at the altar. Dozens of people found Christ that night, and the lives of many Christians were significantly changed.

This reinforced a commitment I had made for myself. I resolved never to be chained to a program, but to be acutely sensitive to the leading of the Spirit! We must commit to flexibility and spiritual sensitivity when we stand in the pulpit.

The Price Required to Achieve a High Christian Goal

The ministry was not meant to be a safe haven for the floundering, or just a comfortable living for ministers. One in ministry must count the cost and pay the price for success as a messenger of God. Effective ministry calls for knowledge, humility and patience.

Especially when accepting a beginning pastorate far below what you see as your ultimate dream. The first charge is a learning opportunity!

The "School of Experience"

Dreams may be lofty and honorable, but the pastor associates with people of humble status. He must truly love his neighbors—both the loving and kind as well as those who persecute the preacher. The pastor must expect to be a target for animosity and misunderstanding. If the Cross is our symbol, we should not expect a soft cushion or be shocked by antagonisms in a life of ministry.

Lean on God

Prayer is the only effective resource that gives strength to forgive those who hurt us and a vision that is larger than our feelings! The apostle Paul expressed this spiritual and emotional agony in Philippians 3:10: "That I may know Him and the power of His resurrection, and the fellowship of His sufferings, being conformed to His death."

The deepest wounds a man of God receives are from his own people! The pastor learns the limits to the trust he can put in others. Human nature, though redeemed, is strange and unyielding. While maturing spiritually, the pastor will be humbled. He will realize that on occasions he could have performed more like a saint than he actually did. The caring pastor must not keep it a secret that he often has to ask God's forgiveness for personal errors. Sainthood requires apology before purity.

Redeeming Every Fragment of Time

John Wesley ministered to those on the bed of sickness and on the couch of prosperity, in the house of mourning and in the house of feasting. Wherever there was a friend to serve or a soul to save, he humbly went. He thought no office too humiliating, no condescension too low and no undertaking too arduous to reclaim the worst of lost humanity. The souls of all people were equally precious in Wesley's sight.

Embracing this goal is the only true road to success we can take in Christ's ministry. Those who watch are not interested in how much we know or how well we preach; but rather, who and what we are, and how faithfully we live. Paul told Agrippa (Acts 26:19) that he was not disobedient to the heavenly vision. Our experience may not be as cataclysmic as Paul's, but we are, nevertheless, God's chosen men and women.

Our goal must be to obey God's call and develop our holy mission. We are marked men and women before both God and men! The heavenly vision is despised by an unregenerate and secular world. It is often misunderstood by worshipers in our churches. Yet, the vision is what keeps us ministering and striving for our goals. Paul called this a divine treasure:

> For we do not preach ourselves, but Christ Jesus
> the Lord, and ourselves your bondservants for Jesus'

sake. For it is the God who commanded light to shine out of darkness, who has shone in our hearts to give the light of knowledge of the glory of God in the face of Jesus Christ.

But we have this treasure in earthen vessels, that the excellence of the power may be of God and not of us. We are hard pressed on every side, yet not crushed; we are perplexed, but not in despair; persecuted, but not forsaken; struck down, but not destroyed—always carrying about in the body the dying of the Lord Jesus, that the life of Jesus also may be manifested in our body (2 Corinthians 4:5-10).

What a magnificent depiction of pastoral life! We do not preach ourselves, but Christ as Lord and we as servants for Jesus' sake! The glorious treasure of the knowledge of Jesus is held in our perishable human flesh and minds, so that the miraculous nature of it is obviously not our own.

Remember, God has not called us to any service or sacrifice that He will not give us the power to perform.

CHAPTER 5

LET GOD SUPPLY THE MIRACLE

God often showed His power or presence by an impressive sign or miracle in both the Old and New Testaments. Jesus said, "And these signs will follow those who believe: In My name they will cast out demons; they will speak with new tongues; they will take up serpents; and if they drink anything deadly, it will by no means hurt them; they will lay hands on the sick, and they will recover" (Mark 16:17, 18).

Other scriptures speak of the believers' power to perform miraculous signs in the name of the Lord. Emphasis has been placed on this act as proof of the genuineness of a ministerial calling. As a young

Christian, I was impressed with this, and I sought God for miracles as a proof of my calling. When they didn't occur often, I wrestled with a false sense of failure. I didn't realize that miraculous changes in people's lives were the greatest miracle I could hope to see! I was overwhelmed by my own inability. I longed to perform a feat that would impress people with my closeness to God.

I didn't realize that these thoughts were unscriptural. Preparing for the sermon one Sunday, I found myself questioning if anything I said would have any meaning to my people—especially since my ministry seemed to lack "impressive" signs. I knelt in my study and confessed to God my sense of inadequacy.

The Spirit of God spoke to me, "Who told you that you were expected to be adequate? You don't need a miracle, you need Me!" My eyes fell on Christ's words in John 15:5: "I am the vine, you are the branches. He who abides in Me, and I in him, bears much fruit; for without Me you can do nothing" (John 15:5).

People didn't say, "We would see a miracle," but "We would see Jesus!" (see John 12:21). The key thought of that morning was, "Without Me you can do nothing!" I began to realize that no matter how diligently I pursued my studies, how faith-filled my prayers or how committed I was to my calling, it was not miracles, but Jesus, that I needed. If I exalted Him, He would take care of the rest!

After all, I would never be the miracle-worker! That is always God's own prerogative. Through His Holy Spirit He will provide miracles when they are needed as signs of His wonder-working presence. Our part is to let listeners know that they can ask for them and expect them. Not long after, a woman in my congregation became desperately ill. Her family feared she wouldn't survive. The church went to prayer, and one of the elders and I visited her in the hospital. We laid hands on her and anointed with oil in the name of Jesus Christ. In a few hours her condition improved and she returned home a few days later. The church knew they had seen a miracle!

> Is anyone among you sick? Let him call for the elders of the church, and let them pray over him, anointing him with oil in the name of the Lord. And the prayer of faith will save the sick, and the Lord will raise him up. And if he has committed sins, he will be forgiven (James 5:14, 15).

Through the years, God has performed a number of obvious miracles in my ministry. I have learned, however, that miracles are not the gospel. They only "follow" the gospel! We are to lift up Jesus, not miracles. "And I, if I am lifted up from the earth, will draw all peoples to Myself" (John 12:32).

Nothing in God's Word indicates that miracles were performed to draw people to Christ. They simply demonstrate that God himself accompanies the preaching of the gospel. The miracles are intended to magnify and glorify our Lord!

Exaggerated emphases are often placed on miracle-working. I've seen signs that advertised evangelistic meetings, promising miracles. Seldom was the name of Jesus in bolder print than the extravagant claims that guaranteed mighty "signs and wonders." People flocked—not to meet Jesus in a redemptive relationship but rather, they came to satisfy their curiosity. They looked for a special healing or some other desired miracle in their lives, even if it were imagined.

Many who are ill rush to such a meeting, hoping for a special healing. God's servant who is officiating is responsible to tell them that without Jesus no one will see or experience a miracle!

In fact, there can be a "religion" of signs and wonders! African witch doctors claim the power to heal, but they worship demons and Satan himself. Demon worshipers experience healings after the witch doctors pronounce incantations over them! These demonic feats intensify the darkness that overshadows their lives.

Humanity's most deadly disease is sin! Only the blood of Christ can cure that terrible malignancy. Confession alone will not cure it; it requires belief in the gospel, repentance of sins and acceptance of Jesus as Lord and Savior. We must present Him to the lost, and leave the working of miracles to take its Scriptural place as a sign following believers. We must encourage believers to follow Jesus Christ instead of the signs.

I have ministered in worship services where healings and other miraculous acts definitely took place. On several occasions, however, I became so caught up in the excitement of the miraculous that I failed to utilize the opportunity that God-given signs had opened to me.

Usually, those who receive healing or a miraculous touch from God are believers. On a few occasions they are like the man at the Beautiful Gate of the Temple (see Acts 3:2-8) who looked at Peter and John, expecting money or some other tangible gift from them. Luke used the Greek word *iasis* in Acts 4:22 to define the healing that took place in response to Peter's words. It is from the Greek verb *iaomai,* which means a miracle based entirely on the sovereignty of God and not requiring any action by the person who is healed.

Acts 3:11 tells us that the man who was healed "held on" to Peter and John, and all the people who had witnessed this event gathered around them—"greatly amazed." We must discourage this same reaction from people who are healed. A genuine miracle of healing may create excitement for both the minister who prayed and the person who received the miracle, but we must not forget to make a Christian disciple of the recipient. God our Father expects us to lovingly and patiently lead lost souls to redemption in Christ.

Usually, an ill person will not reject a compassionate, soulwinning approach. It is our duty to

quietly and calmly ask them about their relationship with Jesus Christ. They may be ill physically, but their spiritual condition before God may
be much more serious. In God's sight they may
even be spiritually dead. Those who respond that
they do not know Jesus as Lord and Savior have
a spiritual illness worse than their physical one.

Unsaved people who come with serious illnesses do
not think about salvation first. They want deliverance!
Many have seldom, if ever, attended a Christian
worship service. They do not understand that repentance of sin is a prerequisite when they come to
God for release from some physical, mental or emotional malady. God is not in the business of healing
desperately ill unbelievers so that they can get back
to the quality of good health that enables them to
continue their unregenerate lifestyles!

At this point we should lovingly and tenderly urge
them to seek forgiveness for their sins as we pray for
their healing. Be constantly alert to the basics of the
Great Commission, which deals first with making
Christian disciples.

Some conduct so-called healing services for nothing but financial gain, thus damaging the simplicity
and purity of the gospel! If we preach a whole gospel
for the whole man, we have to proclaim the fact that
people who believe and follow Jesus can ask for physical healing and expect to receive it. Healing, however, *is* a miracle; and we must let God take care of
miracles!

A revolting experience I once had illustrates what I am saying. An evangelist was asked to take part in a special tent service conducted by another minister. He was not very well acquainted with the man, and didn't know that he tended to emphasize miracles ahead of faith and repentance. I was asked to join them and I did; but if I had known what I was getting into, I would not have been there!

During the latter part of the service my friend was asked to conduct a strong appeal for finances, ostensibly to cover the "high cost of the meeting." I was sitting near the two men after the offering was taken and could not avoid overhearing their remarks. The evangelist asked my friend, "How much did you raise with that offering?" My friend gave him the figure.

The evangelist replied, "That is nothing but chicken feed; watch my smoke!" He went to the pulpit and said, "Many of you have come for divine healing tonight, and because your prayer card was not dated for this evening you could not come forward. However, I have decided to give you a chance for me to pray for your healing right now." He continued, "I know you have brought a generous offering this evening, so every one of you who will come with a $20 bill and put it in my hand will receive my prayer for your healing." Many sincere but innocent people thronged forward, crowding to get in the prayer line.

The evangelist reached out and touched their

outstretched hands, mumbled a short prayer, and loaded his pockets with $20 bills, and even a few $50s! Then he returned to his seat and said, "See, you have to know how fickle some people are if you are going to get their money."

This kind of procedure is nothing short of outrageous blasphemy in the sight of God. Unfortunately, that was not the only case of its kind in those days, and sometimes even in these days! God will powerfully judge such ecclesiastical thievery! In the eternal future, we may indeed be able to watch their smoke!

The objective of God's redemptive work through the vicarious death and confirmative resurrection of His Son, Jesus Christ, was and is the spiritual rebirth of those who were spiritually dead. Physical healing, the leading of the Holy Spirit, living communication with God, and many other blessings are simply additions to the great central fact of spiritual redemption.

While it may be a true miracle, the supernatural healing of our bodies is, at best, only temporary. "It is appointed for men to die once, but after this the judgment" (Hebrews 9:27). This scripture reminds us that no matter how many wonderful and miraculous physical healings we may experience in a lifetime, physical death is an appointment that none of us will avoid unless we live until Christ returns.

On the other hand, spiritual rebirth is a permanent

event! Why then should we place all of our emphasis on a temporary healing and omit spiritual healing and the gift of eternal life? The latter is 10,000 times more important, and a million or more times as long! Avoid attempts to "sell" miracles for the sensational and temporary relief they provide. They are momentary side effects of the gospel. Though thoroughly Scriptural, they nevertheless will come to a predictable end. "For what is your life? It is even a vapor that appears for a little time and then vanishes away" (James 4:14).

Physical healing is one of the miracles that follow the preaching of the gospel, but it is trivial when compared with the eternal character of the Christian faith. Healings or miracles can never eclipse the gift of eternal life through faith in Jesus Christ! As God's ministers to humanity, we must put first things first and keep physical miracles on the level where God's Word has placed them!

I once ministered to a faithful Christian who was dying. When I first visited his hospital bed, he was terribly distraught. "Pastor," he said, "My doctor just told me that my illness is terminal." I spoke with him about what the Bible had to say about death and eternal life, but when I left, he was still greatly disturbed and afraid.

The next day I visited him and found him completely relieved and at peace. "You have a different attitude today," I remarked. "What has changed you? You seem no longer to fear death."

He smiled and said, "In my prayers last night I said to God, 'I am terrified of the word *terminal.*' Then He said to me, 'What are you worrying about? Everyone is terminal!'"

The obvious truth of this fundamental fact of life gave him peace! We must remember that in every case, physical healing is a temporary miracle. In the end, everyone on earth is terminal—even the most saintly among God's own!

CHAPTER 6

ESCAPING THE PERFORMANCE SYNDROME

$\mathcal{W}$e live in a world in which we are judged solely on the basis of our performance. We are paid, honored, and often accepted or rejected on the quality of our performance. As a result, we often tend to judge ourselves on the basis of our own estimate of our performance. I have counseled with pastors who were terribly depressed because they judged themselves as failures.

The truth is that most men would have failed under similar circumstances. The scales were loaded against them from the start! Men and women of God must remember that they are saved and kept by grace! Our standing with God is not based on performance, good works or any other human effort. "For by grace you have been saved through faith, and that not of yourselves; it is the gift of God, not of works, lest anyone should boast" (Ephesians 2:8, 9).

Romans 4:5 clearly states: "But to him who does not work but believes on Him who justifies the ungodly, his faith is accounted for righteousness." Those who "perform" works in order to get to heaven are grossly misled. *GRACE* is **G**od's **R**iches **A**t **C**hrist's **E**xpense! Our salvation was costly to God, but is totally free to all who believe.

His judgment of works does not affect our salvation status with Him. God tests works like this:

> For no other foundation can anyone lay than that which is laid, which is Jesus Christ. Now if anyone builds on this foundation with gold, silver, precious stones, wood, hay, straw, each one's work will become clear; for the Day will declare it, because it will be revealed by fire; and the fire will test each one's work, of what sort it is. If anyone's work which he has built on it endures, he will receive a reward. If anyone's work is burned, he will suffer loss; but he himself will be saved, yet so as through fire (1 Corinthians 3:11-15).

While our works do not affect our standing with God, they will definitely be tested. God's Word speaks of a judgment of works in 2 Corinthians 5:10: "For we [Christians] must all appear before the judgment seat of Christ, that each one may receive the things done in the body, according to what he has done, whether good or bad." It must be clearly understood that the works in this passage refer only to the Christian. They do not apply to the unregenerate.

These verses let us know that while we are saved and kept by the grace of God, the *quality* of our works will bring us either a reward or a tragic loss at Christ's judgment seat. The first and only requirement to qualify for a reward is to belong to Jesus through His redemptive work.

Two men approached a house under construction. One spoke to no one; he simply took his tools and went to work with the other workmen. The second found the foreman, was hired and went to work on the building also. At the end of the day, the first man got nothing because he had not been hired. The second man was paid because he had gone to the foreman and had been put on the payroll. Christians are like the second man. Our names are recorded in His records!

Though we sometimes fail, God knows our hearts and the intentions that motivate us. If the works prove counterproductive in His kingdom, we will lose our reward but not our salvation.

The sense of loss reminds one of a person fleeing a burning building, leaving nothing to show for long hours—or even years—of work. That person's goals were worthless to God's kingdom.

We should be both encouraged and frightened by the prospect of having our works judged. We can be encouraged by the fact that when we make honest, well-intentioned errors, our reward from God will not be affected because our motives were selfless and Christ-centered. A frightening aspect is that if we perform works for our own glory and notoriety, they will be an embarrassment to us before the Great Judge of true, hidden motives. We will suffer the loss of reward.

Though our visible ministry may seem to be genuine and truly self-sacrificing to others, God, who is omnipresent and omniscient, knows *why* we did what we did. We need to ask ourselves: "What are our *motivations* for performing works for Him?" Although redeemed and rescued, our motives are under divine scrutiny. Our salvation may be secure, but future rewards can and will be questioned on the basis of true motivation. Remember Job's observation of the omniscience of God:

> "For His eyes are on the ways of man, and He sees all his steps. There is no darkness nor shadow of death where the workers of iniquity may hide themselves" (Job 34:21, 22).

The final analysis made by God regarding our works depends upon the *attitude* of our hearts. God knows if we were sincere. "For if there is first a willing mind, it is accepted according to what one has, and not according to what he does not have"

(2 Corinthians 8:12). Our true attitude toward serving God is much more important than our accomplishments!

In view of these sobering Scriptural statements, how can we, as God's people, truly examine our motives? The sober fact of self-examination is that in our own heart of hearts we *know* what our basic motives are! They may be veiled from others. Self-righteous pretension is actually a subterfuge for genuine Christian reality. But we are aware of the deceptive game we play, and so is God!

When there is little likelihood that dishonesty will be discovered by others during this earthly pilgrimage, many professing Christians secretly continue on with impunity. However, the judgment of the quality of our lifework will meet us in the presence of God. An all-knowing, all-revealing judgment is coming; no believer will escape it.

He did not seem to understand that this attitude was *presuming* on the grace of God. David asked God to keep him from committing this very sin: "Keep back Your servant also from presumptuous sins; let them not have dominion over me. Then I shall be blameless, and I shall be innocent of great transgression" (Psalm 19:13).

"What, then," I asked him, "are you going to do about your behavior in God's eyes?" "I won't have to meet these people as my judges," he replied, "but I know I will have to meet God. Long before I die I confess my deceptions to God and He will forgive me!"

This man had chosen present, ill-gotten financial rewards above the future judgment he would receive from God. Not only had he lost sight of the Holy Scriptures, in which we are told, "All liars shall have their part in the lake which burns with fire" (Revelation 21:8), but he was guilty of the more heinous sin of presuming on the grace and mercy of God.

> And do you think this, O man, you who judge those practicing such things, and doing the same, that you will escape the judgment of God? Or do you despise the riches of His goodness, forbearance and longsuffering, not knowing that the goodness of God leads you to repentance? But in accordance with your hardness and your impenitent heart you are treasuring up for yourself wrath in the day of wrath and revelation of the righteous judgment of God (Romans 2:3-5).

The hard fact is that anyone who practices this kind of deliberate deception cannot claim to be a Spirit-led believer! It seems certain that he or she never had a regenerating experience and has been "playing Christian" without ever being born-again. Inner transparency and pure-heartedness is the product of true Christian regeneration.

Every one of us will be tempted in many ways. We experience failures for which we need to ask God's forgiveness. But through it all we will know in our hearts whether we are genuinely serving God or simply pretending for the purpose of deceiving others.

The careful development of a religious "performance" is not the manifestation of genuine Christianity. Some may practice this skill and hone it to a fine edge so that the average person does not recognize them as "pseudo Christians." Others may actually believe they are Christians! But let Jesus tell us about this kind of behavior:

> "Not everyone who says to Me, 'Lord, Lord,' shall enter the kingdom of heaven, but he who does the will of My Father in heaven. Many will say to Me in that day, 'Lord, Lord, have we not prophesied in Your name, cast out demons in Your name, and done many wonders in Your name?' And then I will declare to them, 'I never knew you; depart from Me, you who practice lawlessness!'" (Matthew 7:21-23).

We must be participators in the life of Christ! His somber words give a preview of what will one day happen to any Christian caught in this self-deceiving, Christless performance syndrome. It calls for the death of conscience, the sacrifice of inner rectitude and the crucifixion of what we know to be spoken truth!

Certainly we should constantly strive for better productive performance, but not at the price of integrity and truthfulness. Men and women of God should repudiate any form of make-believe with all their hearts. It is not only a self-destructive habit, but it can be devastating to the faith of believers who discover their spiritual leader has been deliberately misleading them.

A minister's flawless technique in the pulpit may be titillating and entertaining to the congregation, but it can be nothing less than false pretension and polished dishonesty. This is "the performance syndrome" in its worst form.

People do not mind good fiction presented as fiction, but they hate a fiction that is declared to be a fact! Acting out either a fictional or factual performance in the basic truth that it is supposed to portray, and for the righteous reasons for which it was produced, can be entertaining and frequently enlightening. But the "performance syndrome" must be avoided at all cost.

CHAPTER 7

THE PERIL OF PRIVILEGE

*F*ew Christian laymen are aware of both the privileges and perils through which the feet of a pastor must find their way. It is almost impossible to avoid judgmental criticism from both inside and outside of Christian fellowship. Looking back over 60 years of ministry, I recognize many of the perils from which God delivered me. However, I did not always realize the importance of the event or occasion at the time.

For those just entering Christian service, as well as all others who are currently involved in it, I raise warning flags to alert you to these hazards.

I want you to be prepared for them and not become entangled with them. The theme of this book is one of caution on various issues I have felt led of God to discuss with you.

A man or woman of God is a highly visible person. Frequently, those in the community and in the congregation have unrealistic expectations of the way the minister should act, speak and feel. In many ways this congregational leader walks a spiritual and social tightrope in the clear vision of parishioners and the world at large.

On the other hand, real privileges accompany the vocation. He is generally looked upon with admiration and respect by those in the congregation who love him. With their encouragement, he can usually weather unfair criticism some will throw at him.

Those who judge the pastor are usually the ones who do not empathize with him. Their judgment is based solely on his doing things differently from the way they would do them if they were in his shoes!

From time to time in my Christian ministry I have become aware that as a preacher of the gospel I have some privileges not available to those in other vocations. On many occasions I am not worthy of these privileges. I try to accept them with humility and grace, but I am not sure I always succeed. I realize the opportunity to make more of these privileges than what is expected.

The pastor has much of the week to himself. If his vision is clear and his divine call is ringing in his ears, he will spend his time profitably for his family and his people. He is unburdened with heavy manual labor, and there is time for various kinds of exercise and relaxation. Used wisely, these can help maintain good physical health.

Sadly, this free time also allows the pastor the opportunity to become a couch potato, overfeeding before the television set! If he does not learn to balance his privileges and perils wisely, he will lose the respect of his people. His shepherdship of them will disintegrate.

> Occasions for greed, arrogance, a sense of self-importance beyond reality, and a sinister invitation to self-worship or self-aggrandizement come with many of these favors.

A pastor must remain constantly aware of his deep spiritual and social responsibilities toward both his parish and the community. Time he spends in dedicated and erudite preparation are crucial to his success!

Years ago I tested some ministerial students in a pastoral theology class, asking them to list five reasons they felt inclined to enter Christian ministry. Most answers were appropriate. One person, however, gave these: *The ministry is an honorable vocation that people respect. It would give me much free time to do things I like to do. It calls for little or no hard physical labor. It would assure me of a reasonable income and provide a residence for my family. It would lift me above the working class and assure me of a timely and good retirement.*

Obviously, the sense of a divine call from Almighty God had never reached him. His entire concept of Christian ministry could be summed up in one word—*privileged.* That young man's problem was not a gross, outward sin; it was a subtle error within his own heart. I had noticed in many pastoral training classes that while others in the class had shed tears of soul passion for the lost at times, he sat quietly, with his head bowed, in a kind of disjointed communion with his classmates.

I had thought that possibly he was simply an unemotional person who did not weep easily. His answers to my questionnaire, however, revealed the true poverty of his heart. In thinking over past ministerial meetings I have attended, I recall returning to my office at times with a sense of futility. Why did I even bother to attend? Something crucial had been missing, but as a young minister I could not figure out what it was.

One day I attended a special seminar conducted by a true veteran of the Cross. We didn't discuss the manifold problems confronting the church. Instead, that battle-scarred soldier led us to look into our own hearts. We began discussing the problems confronting the integrity of our own inner lives and minds. An overwhelming sense of inadequacy swept over us all. We wept on one another's shoulders. Then we reached for the empowering, healing touch of God. We left with a sense of our unique privileges as servants of God.

Suddenly, we were aware of the fact that the ministry of shepherding human sheep involved hard labor, worry, fears and anxieties. On the other hand, we were privileged because we could enter the throne room of heaven as a royal priest for our people. We were privileged to exercise the ministry of intercession in the presence of God. We could identify with the people's sorrows, and weep with them and for them.

We were the privileged who could spend hours searching the Word, gathering spiritual food for our sheep. We were the privileged who could spend our time preparing a message of profound and eternal truth the listeners would understand.

We were brought face-to-face with the fact that we had the unique privilege of standing by deathbeds, holding dying hands and, at the same time, holding the hands of family members who remained after the death angel departed. We *are* a privileged group, we preachers of the gospel!

But what exactly does that word *privilege* mean to us? Do we see our privileges as priestly opportunities to spend time in the presence of the God of eternity on behalf of our people? Do we look at our privileges as occasions for self-indulgence, lazy repose, semi-secular socializing, hours wasted before the television set or mindless daydreaming?

Do our hospitalized people die alone while family members watch in vain for the appearance of a concerned pastor? Do our people know anything about the comfort of a pastoral arm around them during lonely prayer vigils for wayward or hopelessly diseased children? We are the privileged who can be there perpetuating Christ's heart-healing ministry.

In my ministry I have met self-styled preachers who were so intoxicated with their positions of importance that the cries of a lost world and a hurting church never reached their self-centered ears. Still, they let everyone know how "privileged" they were. I believe that God will one day say to them, "I tell you I do not know you, where you are from. Depart from Me, all you workers of iniquity" (Luke 13:27).

We must so treasure our ministerial privileges that we will use them for the purposes our heavenly Father ordained before time began.

CHAPTER 8

THE PERIL OF PROFESSIONALISM

*M*any preachers of the gospel struggle to keep pace with rapid changes taking place in Christendom. Denominationalism as such is disintegrating on many fronts. Self-directed independent congregations, dissatisfied with congregational alignment to established denominations, are moving out and going on their own.

In many cases and for various spiritual reasons, such flights into independence are justified, but where does that leave the pastors of such congregations? They no longer have the supervision that identified them and helped them maintain certain forms of discipline and self-control.

Many sincere and godly men and women in leadership have become involved with such congregational transitions. Consequently, there are considerations that need to be identified for their help and guidance. Self-determination is, in some cases, a blessing and a freeing-up of many issues associated with rigid denominational control. Often, however, new problems and situations arise that Satan uses to influence the so-called liberated leadership.

Along with the euphoria of being one's own person with one's own congregation comes the serious challenge of walking with God in isolated self-discipline. There is no one to encourage private devotion or lonely, disciplined prayer vigil. It must become a spontaneous inner urge in the heart and mind of God's servant.

At the moment the pastor realizes that he alone is the unaccompanied shepherd, he must begin with himself. There is no earthly over-shepherd to support him in his battle against sloth, prayerlessness, professionalism, jealousy or covetousness. Consequently, it is absolutely imperative for him to develop and strengthen his own relationship with his Lord or he will fail! This is the challenge to every shepherd who is leading his flock and is answerable to no one but God.

One of the more deadly trends I have identified is the drift toward perfunctory professionalism by men and women who have tasted the heady wine of complete independence. A certain thrill comes when one realizes that he or she alone can lead the congregation before God's throne.

With the search for wisdom and power to minister comes the temptation to become an independent thinker, feeler and planner for the people. The pastor must ask and answer carefully, "Can I now become the 'professional' guide and spiritual mentor of my sheep?" To counter this temptation to become "professional," every pastor needs to review the divine compulsion that carried him or her into Christian ministry. Ask often, "Am I still being inwardly obedient to the heavenly vision?"

To be "in Christ" before being "in the ministry" is foundational and paramount! The servant of God must see himself as the Bible depicts him—a God-called shepherd of souls. The deeper his discovery of his true self, along with the recognition of his own besetting sins, the less likely he is to regard his calling as a "profession" rather than a ministry. Whether a preacher of the gospel is tied to a denomination or whether he is independent, he must measure up to the apostle Paul's stated qualifications in 1 Timothy 3:1-7:

> This is a faithful saying: If a man desires the position of a bishop, he desires a good work. A bishop then must be blameless, the husband of one wife, temperate, sober-minded, of good behavior, hospitable, able to teach; not given to wine, not violent, not greedy for money, but gentle, not quarrelsome, not

covetous; one who rules his own house well, having his children in submission with all reverence (for if a man does not know how to rule his own house, how will he take care of the church of God?); not a novice, lest being puffed up with pride he fall into the same condemnation as the devil. Moreover he must have a good testimony among those who are outside, lest he fall into reproach and the snare of the devil.

The qualifications of a bishop must be found in every rank of Christian ministry. In 2 Timothy 4:1-5, Paul moved from the general domestic requirements of God's men to their responsibilities concerning the nature of their preaching:

I charge you therefore before God and the Lord Jesus Christ, who will judge the living and the dead at His appearing and His kingdom: Preach the word! Be ready in season and out of season. Convince, rebuke, exhort, with all longsuffering and teaching. For the time will come when they will not endure sound doctrine, but according to their own desires, because they have itching ears, they will heap up for themselves teachers; and they will turn their ears away from the truth, and be turned aside to fables. But you be watchful in all things, endure afflictions, do the work of an evangelist, fulfill your ministry.

The ancient Probationers in Scotland were asked: "Are zeal for the honor of God, love for Jesus Christ and desire to save souls your greatest motives and chief inducement to enter the function of holy ministry?" A minister with these motives will not be incompetent or insensitive!

The man of God must never be self-deceived and

think that he has become the mediator between God and his people. There is only one Mediator and He is Jesus. You and I do intercede for them, but we lead people humbly, not professionally, into the presence of God.

It is much more effective to be a member of the "Order of the Broken Heart" than to be called a "professional preacher." *Professionalism* can be another term for *heartlessness*.

Unless we maintain prayerful sensitivity, we fall into the trap of thinking we have all the pat answers for the problems of our people. We become so knowledgeable in our own estimation that we do not permit the wounded, brokenhearted and emotionally devastated people to finish telling their sad and true story. We cut in on their tearful efforts with our imagined solutions and never demonstrate genuine empathy and sensitivity to their pain.

The remedy for the aloof, businesslike approach of cold, professional ministering is a truly listening heart and the spirit of a servant of God. Our Lord, who knows every human trauma before it can be verbalized, said:

> "Come to Me, all you who labor and are heavy laden, and I will give you rest. Take My yoke upon you and learn from Me, for I am gentle and lowly in heart, and you will find rest for your souls" (Matthew 11:28, 29).

The meekness and lowliness Christ demonstrated must also be demonstrated by us who are

His under-shepherds. We need never expect to rejoice with those who rejoice until we develop enough sensitivity to weep with those who weep. Genuine empathetic weeping is a mystery to the heartless professional.

The One who is "the resurrection and the life" wept beside a grave—a grave from which He would immediately call a man back to life. Knowing the immediate future, Jesus could easily have been amused at the tears of Lazarus' sisters and the group of mourners at that tomb.

Instead, He wept with them because, as the God-man, He sensed the depth of their human sorrow and hopelessness. May God help us as His earthly representatives to avoid the godless chill of professionalism.

Insensitivity is the first sign of professionalism. Coldhearted disinterest on the part of a pastor is soon recognized by the people. Every man or woman of God must bear in mind that even though some of the problems encountered by people and shared with him or her may seem trivial, they are great obstacles to those affected!

Not one time did Jesus turn away from those who approached Him with problems. Even children gathered around Him with excitement and with a sense of being welcomed and loved. God's pastors cannot permit human sin and failure on the part of anyone to make a difference when they respond to needs.

We are mindful of the woman caught in an adulterous affair and taken to Jesus for condemnation. According to the Law, this would have been a cause for stoning her to death (see John 8:5). She may have been so destitute she was forced to resort to prostitution—we don't know. But the coldhearted professional religionists of the day who dragged her before Jesus are examples of the spiritual callousness engendered by professionalism.

A jaded philosophy of religion and a total neglect of responsibility to the sensitive and fragile souls of our human charges can only result in unsympathetic self-righteousness.

As ministers of the gospel we are commissioned to make disciples, lead people into the truths of Christianity and reveal the heart of God to humanity. We are to manifest the compassion and gentleness of Christ, who was so sensitive to people that it was said of Him, "A bruised reed He will not break, and smoking flax He will not quench" (Matthew 12:20).

We must never become so "professional" that we cannot feel the pain and heartache of others! Hurting people are looking for leaders who genuinely care for them and empathize with them in their pain, regardless of what it may be!

The Gospels tell us many times that Christ had compassion for people in His ministry. This referred to both the crowds and individuals. As He ministered, He was at the same time setting an example of Christian ministry for us to follow.

One experienced pastor remarked to his people, "As often as I can, I will have my feet at your doors. But above all things I want to give you my heart in compassionate understanding and love."

With that kind of motive we will never be trapped by the specter of professionalism!

CHAPTER 9

SETTING A GUARD OVER THE MIND

*I*nterest in physical fitness is at an all-time high. Hundreds of Christians have joined health spas, taken up jogging and bodybuilding, and are seriously pursuing every other kind of physical exercise. While we may be winning the "battle of the bulges," we are not doing as well in the battle of the mind. Never has our thought train been so overloaded with garbage as now.

Rotten thinking always leads to rotten living. Today's thoughts are blueprints for tomorrow's behavior. One needs only to pause at any newsstand to discern the depraved mental diet on which the majority of this generation is gorging itself!

Seeing the temptations people face today, we must be concerned about their thought life. No Christian wishes to acknowledge to God or friends that he or she is losing the moral, ethical and spiritual battle of the mind. Guilt causes some to stop attending church, or at least to cut their attendance to a minimum.

As leaders, we must come to grips with this pastoral challenge and try to walk with our people through the valley of temptation. We must remember that they *are* what they *think*: "For as he thinks in his heart, so is he" (Proverbs 23:7). The problem of righteous thinking is something our parishioners struggle with every day. Outwardly they may portray an upright, moral life, but their inner convictions may leave them frustrated.

Today's amoral society bombards people daily with a thousand non-Christian suggestions. Our preaching must teach them to combat evil trends. When we seem oblivious to struggles in this area, we reinforce the belief that spiritual leaders do not experience the same temptations they do, and cannot understand the problems the laity deals with. We must put ourselves in their shoes. Pastoral counseling will awaken us to their struggles.

How do Christians view this tragic picture? How can sincere believers in God keep their thoughts on a higher plane in the seemingly unavoidable atmosphere around them? "Keep your heart with

all diligence, for out of it spring the issues of life"
(Proverbs 4:23). Paul's mental exercise program is
this:

> And God's peace [shall be yours, that tranquil state
> of a soul assured of its salvation through Christ, and
> so fearing nothing from God and being content with
> its earthly lot of whatever sort that is, that peace]
> which transcends all understanding shall garrison and
> mount guard over your hearts and minds in Christ Jesus.
>
> For the rest, brethren, whatever is true, whatever is
> worthy of reverence and is honorable and seemly,
> whatever is just, whatever is pure, whatever is lovely
> and lovable, whatever is kind and winsome and gra-
> cious, if there is any virtue and excellence, if there is
> anything worthy of praise, think on and weigh and take
> account of these things [fix your minds on them]
> (Philippians 4:7, 8, *Amp.*).

Christians can't feed on the garbage portrayed
in some movies, television shows and pornographic
publications, and, at the same time, experience a
wholesome heart and clean thought life. Don't complain about nightmares if you read ghost stories at
bedtime. Flies of temptation swarm around mental
garbage and cesspools of evil.

> [God] will guard him and keep him in perfect and con-
> stant peace whose mind [both its inclination and its
> character] is stayed on You, because he commits him-
> self to You, leans on You, and hopes confidently in
> You (Isaiah 26:3, *Amp.*).

If we walk in the Spirit mentally, we will not be
borne along on changing tides of filthy thinking. Mental

exercise is more important than physical (although some Christians desperately need the latter too!). Each of us must ask ourself daily, "How am I doing on the battlefield of my mind?" The Holy Spirit, speaking to our consciences, will always supply us with a truthful answer.

Satan attempts to keep our minds focused on *doing* instead of *thinking.* The Holy Spirit concentrates on leading us in our thinking so that our doing and behaving will be acceptable also! We cannot worship in Spirit and in truth if we do not think the truth. We cannot speak the truth if we do not think thoughts of truth.

> "A good man out of the good treasure of his heart brings forth good things, and an evil man out of the evil treasure brings forth evil things" (Matthew 12:35).

We must practice God's way of thinking if we expect to experience His peace in our hearts and minds. Remember, however, that *thinking* in the Spirit is the first phase of *walking* in the Spirit.

Many parishioners are guilt-ridden, and deal with thoughts of lust, dishonesty, selfishness and all kinds of immorality. They come to God's house, hoping to find help in judging between good and evil. They want to learn to keep their minds on safer ground, not realizing that men and women in Christian ministry have the same kinds of temptations. God-appointed shepherds, if they will admit it, fight the same tremendous battles of the mind that their human sheep do.

If we acknowledge this, they will ask how we triumph over them. If we have not learned to triumph, how can we advise them? Keep in mind that shared temptations are not shared triumphs unless we teach our followers how to keep their minds on wholesome levels. As pastors of earnest and sincere people who struggle with the problem of a truly Christian thought life, we must ask ourselves, "Have I been able to define the *what* and *how* of my thought life?"

The point that I am making is illustrated in an experience I had. An honest young man called requesting a counseling session. He didn't identify the problem until he came to my office. "Pastor," he said to me, "I am struggling with a sinful and dirty mind."

"Just what do you mean by that statement?" I asked.

"I cannot keep my mind off young women and sex," he replied.

"Are you married?"

"No, but I wish I could find someone who would love me and consent to be my wife."

I could see he was totally confused about the issue of sex. "What kind of a sexual relationship are you dreaming of?" I asked.

"Oh, I'm not sure I know what is normal anymore, but I want a quiet relationship with a happy and loving wife."

"Who do you think put those thoughts in your mind?" I asked. Puzzled, he asked, "Are you saying

God made me think that way?" He finally accepted the fact that God made male and female, and that the most powerful stimulus after basic self-preservation is that of sex. He was relieved to realize that his thoughts about sex and a happy marriage were not evil or sinful but perfectly normal. He was delighted to be set free from a pattern of thinking that had kept him under condemnation for a long time.

From then on I resolved that I would encourage pastoral students and counselors to stop generalizing the term *sin* and do a better job of defining it in the context of human nature. A normal human male—whether a minister of the gospel or a businessman, married or unmarried—will notice a beautiful woman whose sexuality draws his attention. But that does not mean he can lust after her in his heart. Jesus said:

> "But I say to you that whoever looks at a woman to lust for her has already committed adultery with her in his heart" (Matthew 5:28).

Both Satan and the carnal nature may suggest making reality out of our daydreams, but we must rebuke evil of all kinds, especially that of our thought life. Sinful thoughts can be converted into adulterous acts quickly, and may not be dismissed as easily as simple admiration. This may call for the help of the Holy Spirit to help us avoid taking it to its full-blown, evil conclusion.

We who preach the gospel often leave the impression by generalizing so indiscriminately that listeners, especially younger ones, conclude that all sexual thoughts are sin. When we suggest that the normal, powerful, God-given sex drive in youth is sin, we ourselves are sinning against these naive and impressionable minds.

We must define clearly that God had a noble purpose in creating them this way. Otherwise, we leave our confused listeners with the erroneous idea that their only alternative is mental rebellion and unbelief. Recognize that the greatest struggle in reaching mental rectitude and honesty for Christians centers in the battle of the mind. Every single action in which we are involved originates in our mind before it is acted out physically and revealed verbally.

The struggle with hypocrisy is our biggest struggle. It often rages in the mind! It is possible to demonstrate an outward demeanor before others that is either genuine or pretense, while those who observe us may not realize the true one. We alone know the truth, however, and that knowledge is either a source of honest joy or secret shame.

To provide guidance for a triumphant thought life, we must teach people that this inner struggle is actually between the old nature of sin and the new regenerated man. They must be able to distinguish between the thought life of an unregenerate person and a regenerated one. Both struggle with what we call "conscience." Look at Paul's own personal discovery in waging this endless battle within our hearts and heads.

> As it is written: "There is none righteous, no, not one; there is none who understands; there is none who seeks after God. They have all turned aside; they have together become unprofitable; there is none who does good, no, not one." "Their throat is an open tomb; with their tongues they have practiced deceit"; "The poison of asps is under their lips"; "Whose mouth is full of cursing and bitterness." "Their feet are swift to shed blood; destruction and misery are in their ways; and the way of peace they have not known." "There is no fear of God before their eyes" (Romans 3:10-18).

This is a graphic picture of the mind-set of the unregenerate man. It highlights the difficulties the gospel faces in effecting moral and mental redemption. The first lesson to teach is that even regenerated people cannot think victoriously without the moment-by-moment help of the Holy Spirit. The newly born-again person who tries to live an overcoming life without His indwelling power will experience what Paul describes:

> For I know that in me (that is, in my flesh) nothing good dwells; for to will is present with me, but how to perform what is good I do not find. For the good that I will to do, I do not do; but the evil I will not to do, that I practice. Now if I do what I will not to do, it is no longer I who do it, but sin that dwells in me.
>
> I find then a law, that evil is present with me, the one who wills to do good. For I delight in the law of God according to the inward man. But I see another law in my members, warring against the law of my mind, and bringing me into captivity to the law of sin which is in my members. O wretched man that I am! Who will deliver me from this body of death? I thank God—through

> Jesus Christ our Lord! So, then, with the mind I myself
> serve the law of God, but with the flesh the law of sin
> (Romans 7:18-25).

Follow the example of Paul's victorious discovery. The regenerated person who delights in the law of God learns that believers are not only *saved* by grace, but they are *kept* by grace through faith and the power of God. Fleshly nature cannot contribute anything righteous, holy or good. Shepherds of souls must learn to depend wholly on the Holy Spirit. He enables us to fix our minds on Jesus and follow these instructions:

> (For the weapons of our warfare are not carnal, but mighty
> through God to the pulling of strong holds;) Casting down
> imaginations, and every high thing that exalteth itself
> against the knowledge of God, and bringing into captiv-
> ity every thought to the obedience of Christ (2 Corinthians
> 10:4, 5, KJV).

We must accomplish this through the power of the indwelling Spirit, and teach it to our people so that they, too, can experience it. The Greek language in this verse requires careful interpretation. The English term used in the King James Version is *imaginations*. It is from the Greek *logismous*, meaning "sophistries, or deceptively subtle reasonings." This implies more than normal thinking. It speaks of deliberately deceptive teachings that are proclaimed as lofty intellectualism. Godless teachings are emphasized as a wiser and higher philosophy of life, ethics, morality and behavior than Christianity.

Paul declared them to be "against the knowledge of God," in their facade as religious philosophy. The apostle was not speaking to those who indulged in the tawdry immorality of low Corinthian night life! He was speaking to intellectuals whose general philosophy was polytheistic, anti-moral, hedonistic, epicurean, deceptively subtle and diabolically contrived. Those captivated by this deadly philosophy explained away the evil and lawlessness of sin. They were the self-styled "higher critics" of Paul's day. Their present-day disciples are very much alive in the church of Jesus Christ and in modern society.

Verses 4 and 5 speak of more than a casual rejection of this thinking. Paul commands Christians to "overthrow" these ideas, and to bring every one into captivity to obedience to Jesus Christ. This is spiritual *warfare*—hand-to-hand and at close quarters! It is speaking directly to the battle of the mind, because Paul also commands us to bring every thought into captivity . . . to Christ. The mental action spoken of in this passage of Scripture must be Christ-centered and Holy Spirit empowered. Paul gives a step-by-step sequence as to how this battle must be fought in our minds:

1. We are armed with spiritual rather than carnal weapons.

2. Their purpose in our spirit and soul is to enable us to pull down these strongholds of evil.

3. We are to cast down and literally trample under our feet every kind of deceptive reasoning, and every kind of godless, erroneous thinking.

4. We are to capture and conquer every thought and bring it into obedience to Christ!

Paul's strident and militaristic description of this struggle emphasizes the fact that this battle is not a sleepy-time exercise with only half of our mind engaged. It speaks of a hundred percent commitment to disciplined Christian thinking—not just in times of warfare but every moment of every day. The soldier who falls asleep in battle will be a casualty rather than a victor.

In a world of lazy morals and wandering thoughts, many Christians have not conquered but have been themselves conquered by those thoughts. The pastor who is mentally asleep to spiritual warfare may be singing a deadly spiritual lullaby to a dozing Christian congregation! It is time for a clarion wake-up call. We desperately need the active participation and indwelling power of the Holy Spirit to guard our minds.

The unrelenting battle that goes on in the minds of believers does not always concern sexual behavior! *Jealousy* is another evil that grasps the minds of many people and destroys fellowship and Christlike thinking. Solomon declared, "Jealousy is cruel as the grave: the coals thereof are coals of fire, which hath a most vehement flame" (Song of Solomon 8:6, KJV). It has literally immobilized many servants of God.

No two people possess the same giftings, either in talent or capabilities. One of my first Bible college lecturers warned: "If you are not big enough in mind and in spirit to lead someone to Christ whose giftings and talents far exceed yours, you are too small to enter the Christian ministry." Jealousy is often caused by a self-image that is too lofty. Apparently Paul struggled with a self-magnified ego:

> For I say, through the grace given to me, to everyone who is among you, not to think of himself more highly than he ought to think, but to think soberly, as God has dealt to each one a measure of faith (Romans 12:3).

Nothing hinders a servant of God more than jealousy regarding another servant of God who may excel in giftings or certain abilities that he himself does not possess. This demon of jealousy also raises its evil head over material possessions. Our standing before God as His servants is not affected positively or negatively by the cost of the car we drive, the house we live in or the church we pastor. I have seen these things destroy fellowship among some of God's pastors and their spouses. Jealousy is usually the carnal expression of covetousness. Jesus said:

> Take heed and beware of covetousness, for one's life does not consist in the abundance of the things he possesses (Luke 12:15).

I thought of this when I visited the place in Africa where David Livingstone died. He worked most of his life in semi-poverty, but no one ever moved a continent of people from darkness to light the way he did.

Anger and *personal hatred* are demons that attack the minds of God's servants. The first often arises out of religious-political jockeying for positions in the body of Christ. When one gains a position another dreamed of, the latter dislikes—and in some cases, hates—the one who has gained the position. The greatest damage to the family of God is carnal quarreling and bickering between Christian leaders. This evil simply reveals what these persons of positional importance are thinking in their hearts about themselves and others.

If Jesus was tempted in *all* points as we are (Hebrews 4:15), we know that we, His under-shepherds, will experience temptation to the same degree. To fail to let our parishioners know that we experience the same kind of temptation and Satanic attacks in our minds as they do is to play spiritual superman. They soon find out that pretended superiority is nothing less than a farce, and they lose confidence in our unrealistic preaching. It will not help our people if we merely acknowledge that we experience the same temptations as they do. What they want to hear is *how* to triumph over these tough tests.

Example is always a chief ingredient in successful leadership. In addition to being an example to others, we have the great satisfaction in our own hearts and minds that we ourselves have found the practical road to victorious thinking in today's jungle of degenerating morality.

God's servants through the ages have experienced

the great battle of the mind. The psalmist triumphantly declared: "Your word I have hidden in my
heart, that I might not sin against You. Your word
is a lamp to my feet and a light to my path" (Psalm
119:11, 105).

I too have discovered that the greatest antidote to
the poison of evil thinking is to turn quickly to God's
Word and read its enlightening instructions. We who
would lead God's people must be both Christ-centered
and Word-centered!

CHAPTER 10

A Christian Work Ethic

*T*he temptation to neglect the basic work ethic of Christian ministry is abundant and subtle. Ministry is different from other occupations. Ministers don't punch a time clock to start work. No one keeps track of how we invest our hours.

It is understandable, then, that people expect us to spend time in prayer and consecrated thinking, and to study God's Word. They expect us to take time for exercise and recreation. They also hope we've heard the Lord say, "Feed My sheep!" and we take to heart Paul's words: "Be diligent to present yourself approved to God, a worker who does not need to be ashamed" (2 Timothy 2:15).

I know what it's like to try to get alone to prepare a sermon or read a good book. The telephone rings incessantly. A well-meaning friend drops by to discuss an inconsequential matter important only to him. Time thieves are expected. But many of God's ministers are guilty of downright laziness. We do not plan to be lazy, but we allow it to happen. We permit Satan to entangle us in trivia when we should be busy in God's business.

Pastors confess that they are unable to get a handle on the control of their time. Important tasks are postponed by insignificant interruptions. Preparation for crucial issues is pushed into the night after everyone else has gone to bed. By then they are so tired that they are far from their best in preparing the message. Time for prayer and meditation has been subtly stolen.

A pastor must clearly define his schedule so people will know when he or she is comfortably available. Emergencies always demand immediate attention; but the temptation to be lethargic is something against which we must guard. The Bible says, "Go to the ant, you sluggard! Consider her ways and be wise" (Proverbs 6:6).

A deadly by-product of sloth is a raw and gloomy state of mind inclined toward melancholy and despair. I've counseled men of God who were at the point of giving up their ministries because apathy had so defeated them. They had given up hope of gaining control over their time, and their ministry revealed such a lack of preparation and diligence that they were no longer feeding their sheep with the Word of God.

A Turkish proverb states it succinctly, "A busy man is troubled with but one devil, but a slothful man with a thousand."

In "Personne's Tale," Chaucer called sloth a "rotten sinne," and lists serious vices springing from it: negligence, tardiness, slackness, coldness, sluggish nonchalance and procrastination. When precious hours are frittered away with secondary interests and religious fussing over trifles, we succumb to the vice of sloth. And our people soon discover what is happening.

Why is sloth such a deadly sin in the life of a minister? Because one can make an outward show of busyness and respectability, while in his private life he is hopelessly lazy. To work hard for a seminary degree and then permit sloth to paralyze us is like a hunter I knew in Canada. He came home with 10 fat mallards but was too lazy to clean and roast them.

"The lazy man does not roast what he took in hunting, but diligence is man's precious possession" (Proverbs 12:27). God will remove His fresh anointing and blessing from the minister who carelessly fritters away his time all week and then imagines that he can be ready for Sunday morning by spending an hour on Saturday night in the study. He may entertain the congregation, but he will not feed the sheep!

Sloth is almost imperceptible in its initial stages. Like termites working unseen inside the structure of a house, they destroy the life and strength of a magnificent building, causing it to crumble into dust under the pressure of use.

> Idleness is rust and death slow working,
> But work is God's great gift to those not shirking.
> Save us, Lord of Sabaoth,
> From the dread disease of sloth.
>
> Save us from its living death,
> Let our work for You be blest,
> Let the glory of our tasks,
> Help us trust for all we ask.
>
> Teach us the joy of working for You,
> In wearying labor let us be true,
> Give us the end of a soldier brave,
> Reward our tasks with souls You save.
>
> Keep our faces toward our foe,
> Empower our witness as we go,
> Crown our work with the victor's song,
> And teach us to work though the task be long.
>
> —*Unknown*

Sloth wears many faces and some seem so demanding and essential that we make time for them. In looking back over a lifetime of Christian ministry, I have identified a number of things that are forms of sloth, although I did not see them in that light when I was younger. I have found them to be thieves of my time and activities. They cause me to make excuses for what is nothing but laziness.

Gossip and Extraneous Conversation

When preparing a sermon, the servant of God should have no time for small talk (although sometimes a light and momentary diversion relieves tension). Gossip, a thief of time, usually masquerades under the guise of counseling, Christian guidance or essential visitation.

I know many successful pastors and evangelists, as well as skilled teachers. One thing I have noted is that while they are approachable and ready to talk, they don't spend a lot of time doing so! They get straight to the point being discussed, then promptly close the conversation.

To illustrate, my last service in formal ministry was on a pastoral staff under the senior leadership of a successful servant of God. He taught me much, although I was older. He was a man of few and clear-cut responses. In staff meetings he opened with, "Very well, let us get to the point!" Always helpful and compassionate, he was always brief! Gossip was not tolerated, and if anyone had an important report, it had to be presented quickly and accurately. From him I learned that time is a valuable commodity, and we need to learn to spend it wisely. Although a pastor's time can be utterly consumed by worthless chatter, he must be open, wise and approachable.

In and Out Telephone Calls

Trying to counsel people with a telephone call is often a waste of time. The counselor cannot see facial expressions, and is unable to judge the emotional reaction to his questions or observe the sincerity with which the person speaks and reacts. Ten minutes of face-to-face counseling is usually worth an hour on the telephone. The pastor must learn to shorten inconsequential telephone calls without evidencing impatience.

When you originate a telephone conversation, know what you wish to discuss. Be specific and cordial. Encourage the party to respond distinctly, unhurriedly and loudly so that there is no misunderstanding on your part. On incoming calls, kindly ask the caller to speak slowly enough for you to get the message accurately. Give any instructions you have as explicitly, kindly and briefly as possible. When the caller is in another city, give as much time as you can until the problem is clearly in mind. Do what you can to save time, then conclude the call graciously.

I have known pastors to speak for hours on the telephone to people far and near, then complain that telephone ministry takes so much time they cannot prepare their sermons. Which is more valuable—time for study, prayer and preparation, or time wasted in frivolous tongue-wagging? On the other hand, we have to guard against being unapproachable to those who genuinely hurt.

Television

Current events are important. Every pastor should know what is happening in the world. Yet, people in the congregation who are engaged in various vocations are better acquainted with the world than the pastor. He need not spend more time watching television than is absolutely necessary. He is not a news reporter for the people, but a shepherd of their souls.

The pastor is a mediator between his congregation and the secular world. He shares the task of mediator that the Lord has assigned to His shepherds. Television viewing may truly steal time that should be devoted to the spiritual leading of the people. Morally, spiritually and mentally, television is likely to become a time waster rather than a source of information.

The quality of the programs the pastor watches will either inspire him or tempt him, depending upon his choice. Being a pastor does not make a man or woman of God immune to the danger of being dragged down morally. Like many others in the calling, you can degenerate to the level of a television addict.

Without a doubt, television viewing has become one of the most common excuses for laziness. Pastors, guard your souls against this lazy pastime. It has the power to cripple your ministry both in the sight of God and ultimately, in the hearts of your people.

Movies

Some avoid movies; others feel that attending a decent movie is acceptable. Since there are some excellent films with a great message or theme, the decision to see them must be a guarded one for the pastor simply because of the varied judgment that members of the congregation may pass on the films. Once more, the time spent on this activity becomes an issue.

Thank God some companies produce Christian movies. The general consensus is, "Think carefully about what you watch if it has *not* been produced by Christians." We need to ask ourselves seriously, *Is it really essential for me to see this film, or is it a veiled excuse to avoid work? Am I truly following my holy calling?*

Unnecessary Appointments

People talk to their pastor for as many reasons as there are people! The pastor should be as selective as possible in setting up appointments. Hundreds of hours of study and sermon preparation are lost every year by the intrusion of an hour or so of superficial conversation that concerns no particular problem. Every pastor who employs a secretary or receptionist should train that person how to handle this kind of call.

The caller should be identified by the receiving secretary who will tactfully inquire as to the nature of the call. Usually, if the pastor does not have time for the call, it should be directed to a staff member who is chosen and qualified to answer incoming questions. Financial questions may be referred to the business manager; calls concerning illness, to the hospital-visitation minister; doctrinal questions, to the minister of education or a Bible class teacher; and emotional problems, to a counselor.

Only those calls which are for the pastor personally should be routed through to him. The man of God who simply loves to excessively "shoot the breeze" with his people and with local church golfing pals will probably hit only the breeze in his preaching.

Recreation and Physical Exercise

Both of these activities are essential if the pastor is to maintain his or her health. However, they can also become excuses for wasting time. Golf is one of the favorite forms of relaxation for many active pastors. It is a legitimate exercise that may be included in a pastor's weekly schedule. But this, too, must be governed by the workload of the individual.

The same is true of other away-from-the-office relaxation. Set up a realistic schedule. Begin the programmed activities with priorities. Recreational activities are to be ranked on their levels of importance, but include forms of physical exercise.

The sanctuary and church offices should never be left unattended. Time for activities away from the office should be staggered among the staff and support staff. Designating an unnecessary activity as essential is, in fact, a disguised form of sloth.

Family Organization

The family of the pastor has first claim on his time and energies. Some counselors place the church first, but this is out of order. I have known several who put their churches' responsibilities ahead of family obligations and Christian parenting. Most of these men lost all or part of their families to the secular world. Their children grew up literally hating anything that has to do with church. They felt, and often rightfully so, that they had been cheated of time with their father.

In some cases even the mother had been carried away with a form of dedicated fanaticism that deprived the children of the love and parental concern they deserved. In such cases the parents are so busy "serving the Lord" that their behavior may not be considered laziness. Rather, it is a mixture of false piety and misplaced priorities, which is just as damaging.

Yet, the family must understand that a serious-minded pastor must have private time for prayer, study and sermon preparation. Unfortunately, some pastors' spouses and families are not understanding in this regard. I recall a wife who was ridiculously demanding. She compared her husband's work with that of other men's and insisted that her husband attend to any number of trivial activities. On Saturday, she wanted him to pattern his activities after those of her friends' husbands who enjoyed a day off from their regular jobs. She wanted Saturdays for social activities, ignoring the fact that sermons should be prepared as close to the time of public presentation as possible.

She did not understand the loss of concentration and focus that occurs if too much time intervenes between preparation and presentation. In such cases, the pastor may have to prepare some of his message ahead of time, and yield at least part of Saturday for family activities. The point is the family should use a modicum of give-and-take in these matters. All may have to sacrifice in order to achieve consideration for everyone in the family.

Anything we permit to take priority over God's service is, in fact, a person-centered decision and can be designated as slothful if the family is too apathetic to deal with it. Family prayers and the family altar must be maintained at all costs!

The Question of Adequate Sleep

Sleep is a divine provision that enables us to maintain the blistering schedule some pastoral households have to observe. There is a thin line, between enough sleep and deliberate laziness. An old adage declares, "Early to bed, and early to rise, makes a man healthy, wealthy and wise." This is true in a pastor's schedule. One cannot watch television until 2 a.m. and expect to be alert enough in the morning to think with God!

A reasonably early but flexible retirement hour must be set in the pastor's household. Successful pastors are often early risers because morning is when we do our best work. I think more clearly and find personal communion with God most alive and real in the mornings. The pastor's family will rule time as their servant, or they will allow time to rule them.

> See then that you walk circumspectly, not as fools but as wise, redeeming the time, because the days are evil. Therefore do not be unwise, but understand what the will of the Lord is (Ephesians 5:15-17).

CHAPTER 11

THE FUTILITY OF FRETFULNESS

*P*salm 37 is one of the most beautiful of all that flowed from the pen of King David. Certainly he had endured stead-fastly the enmity of those who hated him and were jealous of him. Evildoers were a constant threat to him and to his dream of solidifying Israel as a nation under faith and under divine direction. In the opening verse, David made two distinct ob-servations. He counseled against fretfulness when we see the behavior of evil people, and he warned against envying them in any way.

Do not fret because of evildoers, nor be envious of the workers of iniquity. For they shall soon be cut down like the grass, and wither as the green herb. Trust in the Lord, and do good; dwell in the land, and feed on His faithfulness. Delight yourself also in the Lord, and He shall give you the desires of your heart. Commit your way to the Lord, trust also in Him, and He shall bring it to pass. He shall bring forth your righteousness as the light, and your justice as the noonday. Rest in the Lord, and wait patiently for Him; do not fret because of him who prospers in his way, because of the man who brings wicked schemes to pass. Cease from anger, and forsake wrath; do not fret—it only causes harm (Psalm 37:1-8).

I was traveling on a fund-raising program for our denominational missions board after a 10-year mission assignment in Southern and Central Africa. A promotional meeting was scheduled for a weeknight. When I arrived, the pastor was meeting with the town council. The church wanted to acquire a plot of ground for a new building. Shortly after I got there, he came back to the parsonage greatly distraught.

The council had turned down his request on a flimsy excuse that was prejudiced against Christianity. One had remarked that the plot he wanted for a new church was sought by others who wanted a liquor store and dance hall. I asked if anyone on the council was a Christian. He said he doubted that any of them had any interest in the gospel or the church.

"What would you expect from a group of men David

would have classified as 'evildoers'?" I asked him. Then I reminded him of David's words nearly 3,000 years ago and the futility of fretting over the action of these unbelievers. He began to calm down, and remarked that he had forgotten he was dealing with people whose motivations were political and financial, not something godly.

Active pastors often encounter similar situations. Anti-Christian sentiment is growing rapidly in some areas of our country. If we permit this godless action to create a peevish, perverse spirit in our hearts, it will hurt deeply. It doesn't help our association with the community outside the church, and weakens our influence and ministering authority within the church body.

Bear in mind that we are to pray for those who spitefully use us. We are to demonstrate the long-suffering of God toward them. In some ways, the pastoral family lives in a glass bowl under the scrutiny of all kinds of people, both good and bad. To let our lights shine before men is one of our toughest assignments. If we forget this, we weaken our impact for Christ in the community.

The irreligious and self-centered actions of people who do not know God will always be frustrating and discouraging. Fretting about them, however, is counterproductive if we want to lead these people to Christ. In the above verses David gives us seven ways to handle such situations:

---

1. Don't fret about what godless people do or say.
2. Trust in the Lord, and do good.
3. Delight yourself in the Lord and watch Him fulfill your desires.
4. Commit your way (including the grievous matters) to the Lord.
5. Rest in the Lord and wait for Him to bring your desires to pass.
6. Stop being angry, forsake wrath or the desire to get even.
7. Don't fret; it only causes harm to yourself and others!

Satan tries to get us angry at the people for whom we are praying and attempting to lead to Christ. We must let our light, not our anger, shine before unregenerate humanity. *Fretting*, a term for *worry*, produces stress. It has caused more heart attacks than most other problems. Cherish the promise: "Casting all your care upon Him, for He cares for you" (1 Peter 5:7). *Worry* is an insidious trap. We find ourselves concentrating on problems. We think that all sorts of things, manufactured by our own imagination and blown out of all proportion, *may* go wrong. Trusting Him is easier said than done.

> Casting down imaginations, and every high thing that exalteth itself against the knowledge of God, and bringing into captivity every thought to the obedience of Christ (2 Corinthians 10:5, KJV).

The Greek word for *thought* (*noema*) means "a

perception or dream that was essentially bad . . . an evil expectation . . . an evil design." It was used by Paul in this context and speaks of the great stress that comes from focusing on things that cause worry. For the pastor of God's sheep, there is enough stress in simply fighting the great battle of faith and righteousness! To add this risky dimension to our future designs and dreams may destroy both them and us! This is why Paul commanded us to bring every thought into captivity to the obedience of Christ. If we are worried and under pressure regarding a plan, a design or a dream that seems in danger of failure, we should carefully examine the true spiritual nature of the dream itself.

I have prayed with more than one pastor who was broken and confused because his personal dreams for advancement were not being realized. They were based not on the humility of Christ, but rather on political maneuvering, unhealthy spiritual relationships and carnal desires for ministry beyond both the person's maturity and intellectual capabilities.

> For I say, through the grace given to me, to everyone who is among you, not to think of himself more highly than he ought to think, but to think soberly, as God has dealt to each one a measure of faith (Romans 12:3).

Dissatisfaction and worry about our ministries and places of service are easily discerned by our people. In counseling younger pastors, often I have discovered that the major problem was impatience. They were doing well for their age, experience, talents and training; but expectations had been slower in coming to reality than they had hoped. Impatience over the pace of salary growth and jealousy of others more successful than they also galled them. Paul told these people to bring their imaginations and every carnal thought into obedience to Christ's humbling call.

The Bible declares that the laborer is worthy of his hire.

> "And remain in the same house, eating and drinking such things as they give, for the laborer is worthy of his wages" (Luke 10:7).

> The Scripture says, "You shall not muzzle an ox while it treads out the grain," and, "The laborer is worthy of his wages" (1 Timothy 5:18).

Worthiness is demonstrated by one's success in winning souls and ministering grace. I have gone into new and strange places with simple gospel preaching, and have been welcomed into poor homes—sometimes those of widows. I have always been adequately cared for. If a pastor truly feeds the sheep, they will take care of the shepherd and the work will grow. One of Christ's most emphatic messages is on worry:

> Then He said to His disciples, "Therefore I say to you, do not worry about your life, what you will eat; nor about the body, what you will put on. Life is more than food, and the body is more than clothing. Consider the ravens, for they neither sow nor reap, which have neither storehouse nor barn; and God feeds them. Of how much more value are you than the birds? And which of you by worrying can add one cubit to his stature? If you then are not able to do

the least, why are you anxious for the rest? Consider the lilies, how they grow: they neither toil nor spin; and yet I say to you, even Solomon in all his glory was not arrayed like one of these. If then God so clothes the grass, which today is in the field and tomorrow is thrown into the oven, how much more will He clothe you, O you of little faith?

"And do not seek what you should eat or what you should drink, nor have an anxious mind. For all these things the nations of the world seek after, and your Father knows that you need these things. But seek the kingdom of God, and all these things shall be added to you.

"Do not fear, little flock, for it is your Father's good pleasure to give you the kingdom. Sell what you have and give alms; provide yourselves money bags which do not grow old, a treasure in the heavens that does not fail, where no thief approaches nor moth destroys. For where your treasure is, there your heart will be also" (Luke 12:22-34).

I remember when my wife, Merle, and I faced what was to be our first experience of poverty. Our first pastorate was near both her parents and mine. They lived on farms 10 miles apart, and when we ran low on groceries we could drive about 40 miles and fill the trunk of our little Ford with plenty of food. Soon, our little church rallied to meet our needs, and their offerings and gifts kept us supplied.

Then the superintendent of the area moved us to a city to produce a series of radio broadcasts. The denominational office was able to contribute only $20 per month. One morning Merle said,

"This cereal is all we have, and when it is gone we will be out of food!" Since both of us had been raised on good farms, it was the first time either of us had faced the sobering prospect of having nothing to eat! "But," she said, "God knows how things are with us, so we will pray right now for some food!"

I have always felt that my wife has more practical faith than I have. We prayed. I must confess that my thoughts were on the nearby grocery store. Many doubts assailed me! In an hour there was a knock on the door. One of our church members said, "This morning as I was shopping, the Lord told me to buy double items—one for your family and one for my family!"

As soon as he left, with our thanks ringing in his ears, Merle and I fell to our knees. Her prayer was one of thanksgiving, mine a mixture of confession, repentance, and a deep sense of gratitude to God for His loving care. Seldom after that experience did we ever come near that level of poverty. Through many years of ministry, both in foreign countries and in the United States, we've seen God provide our needs when resources were limited.

We taught our children to trust God, and had opportunities to demonstrate to them God's great faithfulness. Once in Africa, Merle had an occasion to show them how God really cares. I was gone for a month, traveling to various missions. I thought I had left enough cash for Merle and our three children, but an unexpected expense almost exhausted her funds. With nothing left with which to buy food, she and the children faced an empty table. She put a mustard seed in a tiny jar, and reminded the children of the Lord's promise:

> "Assuredly I say to you, if you have faith as a mustard seed, you will say to this mountain, 'Move from here to there,' and it will move; and nothing will be impossible for you" (Matthew 17:20).

She and the children prayed. Shortly afterward there was a check in the mail from a man who had owed us for so long we had given up hope of ever being paid. He apologized for the delay and paid his debt. This kept the family fed until I returned home and our next mission check from the United States arrived.

Let me encourage you, my fellow Christian minister, by reminding you that God has promised to supply all of our needs, but not all of our wants! We make the mistake of sometimes spending more on our wants than we should. Then we have to scrape the bottom of the cash barrel to survive. I have done that a few times, and on several occasions close friends who knew about my temporary indiscretion reminded me that I had spent our meager cash on things besides our needs.

Parishioners know more about our situation than we think they do, and they certainly help in the lean times. A parishioner casually asked me me one day: "Pastor, how are you getting along?" I replied, "We're getting along all right; why did you ask?" He was not a man of wealth, but he said, "Well, you are my pastor and I've promised myself that the only time you will be hungry will be when my family is hungry too."

If you and I are content to live on the same economic level as our people, they will care for us. They know whether we are laborers worthy of hire. If we truly trust God to meet our needs, they will have the courage and spiritual commitment to do the same. If we exhibit worry and stress, they lose faith and complain about God's failure to meet their needs.

God is not responsible for senseless credit card overexpenditures. Credit cards are *not* God's way of meeting needs. Trust God to care for you according to your income, lest He cause your income to counterbalance your extravagance.

CHAPTER 12

THE ANATHEMA OF AVARICE

*T*he dictionary defines *anathema* as the "denunciation of anything that is accursed." In the Bible it refers to anything God has designated as "cursed." Christian believers must consider the person or thing accursed if God has declared it to be. When the term is applied to humans, it means those whose total rejection of God is so intense that He has given them up to their own atheistic decisions about Him and His existence.

Paul used this term to refer to those who choose not to love the Lord Jesus Christ: "If anyone does not love the Lord Jesus Christ, let him be accursed [anathema]. O Lord, come [Maranatha]!" (1 Corinthians 16:22).

Paul didn't use the Greek word *agape*, which means supernatural, divine love. Instead, he used the Greek word *phileo*—human affection. They refused to love Christ on the supernatural level of God-given love and also on the human level of intellectual and emotional affection. The phrase *anathema Maran atha* is Aramaic, the common language and basic vernacular of the eastern Mediterranean at the time of Paul's writing. He used it to emphasize the state or condition of those he referred to as being under a curse!

Avarice is insatiable greed and covetousness so profound that it is the dominant drive in those who claim to worship God, but worship mammon! It is best defined as "money lust." Unfortunately, money is of primary importance in the minds of some professing Christians! Note Paul's powerful identification of those who had been left under the curse of abandonment by God:

> And even as they did not like to retain God in their knowledge, God gave them over to a debased mind, to do those things which are not fitting; being filled with all unrighteousness, sexual immorality, wickedness, covetousness, maliciousness; full of envy, murder, strife, deceit, evil-mindedness; they are whisperers, backbiters, haters of God, violent, proud, boasters, inventors of evil things, disobedient to parents, undiscerning, untrustworthy, unloving, unforgiving, unmerciful (Romans 1:28-31).

Covetousness is cited as a sin that placed these evildoers under the anathema of being abandoned by God. It is a spiritual tragedy that many believers do not seem to realize this danger. Striving for financial gain at the cost of others seems to be acceptable to some. Paul wrote of the . . .

> useless wranglings of men of corrupt minds and destitute of the truth, who suppose that godliness is a means of gain. From such withdraw yourself. . . . But those who desire to be rich fall into temptation and a snare, and into many foolish and harmful lusts which drown men in destruction and perdition. For the love of money is a root of all kinds of evil, for which some have strayed from the faith in their greediness, and pierced themselves through with many sorrows (1 Timothy 6:5, 9, 10).

In the early years of my ministry I met R.G. LeTourneau, designer and manufacturer of huge earthmoving equipment. He often spoke of God's financial blessings on him and his company, and told his story. During World War II the United States government needed earthmoving equipment to build airfields in the Pacific. Mr. LeTourneau was scheduled to fly to a small town to speak at a new church dedication.

Just before takeoff, his chief engineer approached him and said the U.S. Air Force had submitted an urgent request for a special-design earthmover and urged him to cancel his plans. He replied, "I will trust God to give me the design while I am flying to that church dedication." When the plane took off, LeTourneau prayed, "God, You know how important that machine is and how urgent the need is to our country. Please give me the design for that earthmover." Mr. LeTourneau told me, "A design I had not thought of before flashed into my mind. I quickly drew a rough sketch of it. On the way home, more of the details flashed into my mind and I was able to place the finished mock-up of the machine in the hands of my chief engineer the next morning! Soon afterward we got the contract to build the earthmovers."

I said, "Sir, you are obviously a man of considerable wealth. How do you handle the stewardship of such income?" He replied, "It is not a matter of how much of my money I give to God, but of how much of His money I keep for myself and my business."

Later I discovered that he gave 90 percent of his wealth to the Lord's work, and kept only 10 percent for himself and his family! He made his son shovel snow on college sidewalks at 50 cents an hour to earn his own spending money.

Some of the greatest wounds suffered in the body of Christ have been caused by highly visible, professing Christian ministers who have been indicted publicly for gross avarice. How careful we must be to guard against this common human failure. All of us like comfortable living, money for leisure and relaxation, and the simple possession of more than basic needs. Paul did not say that money itself was the root of all evil. He did declare, however, that the *love* of money was the problem.

Years ago I visited a man who had planted a

number of fruit trees. Some appeared lush and green while others were fading in color and obviously dying. When I asked what was wrong, he said that a root-rotting disease had gotten into his orchard and was killing the trees. "They look normal for a while," he said, "then they suddenly lose color and die." I thought, *That sounds like the story of some of God's servants I have known.*

I thought of ministers, Bible teachers, missionaries who started out with no apparent desire for worldly gain—and flourished in the Lord's work. In time, they either ruined their ministry or gave it up entirely because of covetousness. They fell into the trap of worshiping mammon instead of God.

A man I visited had begun his Christian service almost in poverty. His ministry had blossomed and the obvious blessing of God was upon him. Years later, he fell heir to an unexpected fortune. When I visited him again he was still a person of charm and graciousness, but the things he treasured had changed him. The humble, unworldly servant of old had completely disappeared, and in his place was a man with a sinister spirit of avarice that seemed to leave God out of his life. All he talked about was temporal possessions.

No one among us is immune to this enticement. As the congregation grows, our income usually grows with it. The temptation to be unaccountable is in direct proportion to the level of our financial independence. Billy Graham's ministry could certainly have kept his income secret from the public. Instead, he has proven to be a leader in Christian accountability by dealing openly and transparently with money. A group of Christian businessmen handle the Billy Graham Evangelistic Association's finances. Billy receives a salary with no perks.

When love for money slowly and insidiously takes over and replaces our love for God, tragedy is in the offing for us all. Jesus warned:

> "No one can serve two masters; for either he will hate the one and love the other, or else he will be loyal to the one and despise the other. You cannot serve God and mammon" (Matthew 6:24).

If our love for God and His Son is foremost, we will make mammon our servant instead of our idol. Solomon's answer for everything was money: "A feast is made for laughter, and wine makes merry; but money answers everything" (Ecclesiastes 10:19). He was speaking of material needs, but we must keep the real meaning in mind.

Money is necessary for extending the gospel. Without it, churches cannot be built, local programs cannot be set up, and many facets of evangelism and missionary outreach cannot be initiated. Dr. James Bruce, a spiritual mentor, said, "Raising money for any worthwhile project in the kingdom of God is honorable, Scriptural, moral and spiritual—unless we start to worship the filthy stuff as one of our private gods."

We must keep our love for God pure and untainted by money love. Let's be sure to make mammon our servant for the glory of God. A poor man's "little" can be his god just as can a rich man's "much." Where our treasure is, there will our heart be. Let us pile up treasure in heaven and be content in the condition we find ourselves. Our loving heavenly Father has promised to provide our needs, not our wants.

> Not that I speak in regard to need, for I have learned in whatever state I am, to be content: I know how to be abased, and I know how to abound. Everywhere and in all things I have learned both to be full and to be hungry, both to abound and to suffer need. I can do all things through Christ who strengthens me (Philippians 4:11-13).

Missionary work in Africa taught me a great deal. The roads were almost nonexistent, and the area was poor where one of God's African Christians pastored a small flock of jungle dwellers. I always carried a bag of cornmeal and other staples with me, and when I arrived at his hut, I noticed that both he and his wife looked thin and gaunt.

We were greeted with enthusiasm, but we had not talked long until his wife said in an African tongue: "Missionary, do you have some food? My husband and I have not eaten for three days. Our food supply ran out and it is the dry season here."

They were far from developed towns and they lived on the barter system, but they had nothing to barter. I unpacked the cornmeal and other food and she went to work preparing it. They ate ravenously—and didn't say another word about their poverty. Rather, they rejoiced in their success in winning pagan people to Jesus Christ!

I asked if they would like to move to a place where conditions were better, and they tearfully refused. God had led them to this place of service, and they would not think of leaving. I thought of complaining pastors in America who probably threw out more unused food than these two servants of God had seen in months! They had learned to live as the apostle Paul lived.

When one thinks of this kind of commitment, wrangling among servants of God about salary levels seems almost blasphemous. Paul's words should sober those who are in Christian ministry:

> Godliness with contentment is great gain. For we brought nothing into this world, and it is certain we can carry nothing out. And having food and clothing, with these we shall be content" (1 Timothy 6:6-8).

CHAPTER 13

THE CRUX OF CHRISTIAN COUNSELING

*A*ccording to the dictionary, the word *counseling* is the act of giving professional advice. That guidance may be financial, spiritual, domestic, parental or any other recommended behavioral instruction. The word *crux* implies the determinative point at issue or the central feature of the process.

Scripture speaks clearly of the importance of counseling. During the past 20 years, it has become one of the most important functions of the Christian ministry. No man or woman of God is deemed ready to take oversight of a flock of God's human sheep until he or she has received intensive training in the counseling ministry. To underscore the importance of Christian counseling, we need to recall one of the great messianic prophesies. The prophet Isaiah said, "[Jesus'] name will be called Wonderful, Counselor. . ." (9:6).

Proverbs 24:6 declares, "In a multitude of counselors there is safety." Jesus promised the ministry and presence of the Holy Spirit as "Comforter," which is simply another phase of counseling. Christian leadership recognizes the crucial place of dependable godly counsel in the difficult situations that arise among God's people.

In recent years of my ministry, counseling has become one of its most rewarding phases. If we teach believers to look to the Holy Spirit for comfort and guidance, they will experience His marvelous reassurance and leadership. The Greek word for "comforter" is *parakletos* and means "one who is always alongside to help and direct." As Christians we too are to be comforters.

> Blessed be the God and Father of our Lord Jesus Christ, the Father of mercies and God of all comfort, who comforts us in all our tribulation, that we may be able to comfort those who are in any trouble, with the comfort with which we ourselves are comforted by God (2 Corinthians 1:3, 4).

Part of our ministry is to encourage and reassure one another. We must look constantly for opportunities to exercise this person-to-person ministry. The performance of this service presents some serious pitfalls and grave dangers, however. Two basic questions that must be asked: (1) Is the advice we give truly Biblical—does it line up with Scripture? and (2) Is it practical and workable?

No novice in Christian living can look on himself or herself as a genuine counselor. For example, how can one who has not yet had children be a dependable adviser to those who are experiencing family problems? Gray hair is one mark of graduation from the tough school of experience. Those who seek counsel on how to live need to talk to people who have been around long enough to know something about living.

If we look on academic degrees as absolute qualifications for counseling, we must bear in mind that some strong congregations have perished by "degrees" because those who possessed them knew nothing about godliness or true spirituality. As leaders and shepherds of God's people, we must study to be approved in the counseling field too. Most courses in science provide both theory and lab experiments for total learning. Adequate development in Christian ministry calls for learning *and* experience; however, the "university of experience" provides the final graduation exercise for those in pastoral ministry.

Another factor is dependency. If believers become dependent on their counselor rather than on God, the counselor is not doing his or her duty. Years ago a woman came to me and said, "My counselor keeps telling me to reach down inside of myself and summon up the courage and fortitude to handle my problems." Then she remarked sadly, "I do not have anything like that left inside, so I have nothing to draw upon."

I was able to help her understand God's grace and His resources which would help her rise above her difficulties. She conquered her guilt and defeatism, and was able to find the faith and hope that enabled her to gain victory in her life.

During the so-called Dark Ages, the church became too nosy in its counseling. The clergy learned more than they could be trusted with. Unsuspecting believers found themselves faced with paying bribes to the clergy or risk being exposed to the public or magistrates and the law. Martin Luther rebelled against these evil "indulgences," and brought in the Reformation.

Pastors are not people to whom confessions are made in order to obtain forgiveness. The counselor who can weep with his counselees will be trusted with deep confidences, but that does not make him the believer's confessor! A common ploy used by counselors today is to blame this generation's problems on parents and grandparents who are deceased and cannot be confronted. While parental influence is formative and critical, all of our problems are not hereditary or parental in origin. Each is the sum total of what other people besides our parents have taught us and modeled for us.

Dependable psychological research indicates that we are the human product of inherited genetic predisposition, as well as learned behavior from our family and origin. When we gain maturity, we are expected to recognize some of the errors which we have been taught and to reject them. If we are unable to accomplish this alone, we should gain professional help to modify our unacceptable behavior.

We can learn how to walk in the power of the indwelling Holy Spirit, rather than in the fleshly desires of our old nature. Hopefully, we will have enough sense to stop sucking our spiritual thumbs when we see it pale and undeveloped!

I remember the words of a highly respected Christian counselor who spoke with the authority accorded him by a couple of earned doctorates, plus many years of Christian ministry. He said that good counseling was usually common "horse sense." When asked what he meant by that, he replied, "Horse sense is that rare wisdom in horses that keeps them from betting on men!"

The crux of Christian counseling is the motivation for genuine ministry to others in specific problems. The counselor must have a listening heart and mind. He or she does not need to know more about the counselee than is necessary to understand the situation accurately. Only enough information to administer proper

Biblical, emotional and intellectual guidance is required.

Everyone is born under sin and has sinned. It is not necessary to elicit a detailed résumé of the person's sins. That is really none of our business. It is God's business alone, and He can solve it only through the person's recognition of Christ's substitutionary death on his or her behalf! Our counseling task must deal with the current problem the counselee is facing.

When we interrogate a counselee regarding suspected parental or hereditary problems before we attempt to uncover the current ones, we become confessors, not counselors. The heart of the gospel message declares, "Where sin abounded, grace abounded much more" (Romans 5:20). Our counseling must be based on the proclamation of the grace of God that sets people free of their past and turns their faces toward God's eternal plans for their future.

To counsel another only to uncover that person's past sins and weaknesses reveals a godless objective. The Bible declares, "Therefore, if anyone is in Christ, he is a new creation; old things have passed away; behold, all things have become new" (2 Corinthians 5:17). The task of "becoming new" is immediate in our standing with God; but in our inner experience it is usually a drawn-out struggle. Paul described his own life:

> Not that I have already attained, or am already perfected; but I press on, that I may lay hold of that for

which Christ Jesus has also laid hold of me. Brethren, I do not count myself to have apprehended; but
one thing I do, forgetting those things which are behind and reaching forward to those things which are
ahead, I press toward the goal for the prize of the
upward call of God in Christ Jesus (Philippians 3:12-
14).

Paul is an example to every man and woman in
Christian ministry. Growing in grace is not an acci-
dent. It is a lifelong process of learning to understand our complete self as a new person in Christ,
and learning to understand those whom we counsel and guide.

Unless I can be a man of God and learn the pathway to inner triumph of mind and spirit, I cannot
lead anyone else into it! Forgetfulness of the past
sinful lifestyle is a sacred gift of God's grace. The
writer of Hebrews spoke of this mind-set in the believer when he quoted God as saying, "Their sins
and their lawless deeds I will remember no more"
(10:17).

When I counsel with a person who has accepted
Christ as his Savior, I do not need to go fishing in
the squalid sea of his or her past where "No Fishing" signs have been posted. I have no right to dig
up the sordid deeds of a wicked yesterday. The
sins of those dark days are under the blood of
Christ and buried in the sea of God's profound forgetfulness by grace.

Our omniscient heavenly Father knows all our

sins, and He reveals them to no one. Let us not try to investigate God's secrets under the guise of Christian counseling.

CHAPTER 14

THE TERROR OF BECOMING A CASTAWAY

New church members know of the inner struggle many preachers and pastors face in their private lives. I have counseled with many clergy, not all of whom were young, but who were convinced they were total failures in the ministry. They were ashamed to leave their posts abruptly, but some were sorely tempted to do so. They were afraid that while running in the marathon of leading and ministering to people, they would end up as castaways.

I recall tearful nights when, as a young pastor, I came home from Sunday services feeling like my ministry that day had been empty and fruitless. After some years when I was no longer so young, I still sometimes felt the same depressing feeling. I felt that I had not touched the heart or mind of even one of my parishioners.

One day it finally dawned on me that my responsibility was to "preach the Word" and leave the results to God. After all, He was responsible for the results. Only He can see results anyway. This was what the apostle Paul told his young friend, Timothy: "Preach the word! Be ready in season and out of season. Convince, rebuke, exhort, with all longsuffering and teaching" (2 Timothy 4:2). Our part is to be faithful regardless. "It is required in stewards that one be found faithful" (1 Corinthians 4:2).

I've wondered what kind of discouraging situation the apostle Paul was going through when he wrote to the Corinthian church: "But I discipline my body and bring it into subjection, lest, when I have preached to others, I myself should become disqualified" (1 Corinthians 9:27). Consider the context: Paul is not expressing fear of ejection from the body of Christ or from the salvation wrought in our Lord Jesus Christ. The effectiveness and quality of service is under review.

Christian ministry is like an athlete who endlessly strives for a better score or time. No servant of God wants to be so ineffective that he is merely "beating the air," or "running in uncertainty" (see 1

Corinthians 9:26). We know that our archenemy, the devil, is constantly doing his best to persuade us that such is the case.

Most of God's best men and women experience seasons of depression and frustration. There was a time in my ministry when, after a wonderful season of prayer and communion with the Lord Jesus, I felt so unworthy that I feared I was in danger of becoming a castaway. My vision of the holiness and majesty of my Lord was so profound that my own limitations and weaknesses were glaringly obvious to me. I wondered, *Did Jesus really call me into His ministry?* I felt much unlike a saint! Then I remembered Paul's calling:

> I became a minister according to the gift of the grace of God given to me by the effective working of His power. To me, who am less than the least of all the saints, this grace was given, that I should preach among the Gentiles the unsearchable riches of Christ (Ephesians 3:7, 8).

The great apostle's sense of spiritual weakness and human limitation was such that he faced an incessant fear that he might be running in vain. Maybe too, he feared that some mistake he might make would disqualify him from the prize, and his work would be for naught.

One event in my ministry is burned forever in memory. I had been asked to speak at an important meeting, and had spent much time preparing for the occasion. After the service I experienced a sense of abject defeat. One of my mentors was present and I went to him with a deep sense of having missed the ball entirely. He put his arm around me and said, "Do not be too hard on yourself. No servant of God is so proficient that he performs his duties with absolute perfection! Remember, the fingerprints of your limited humanity can be found on even your best works!"

Too many of us readily become Elijahs under our own particular juniper trees. We begin to feel we are completely alone in our struggle to succeed. The fact is that we are certainly not alone, literally hundreds of God's men and women like us are fighting the same battle.

John Mark is a New Testament example of a would-be assistant minister who seemed to fail after an excellent beginning. As we look at him, we wonder: *Was it fear, ill health, the threat of bodily danger or homesickness that caused him to run back to Jerusalem? Was it cowardice or a haunting fear of youthful inadequacy?* We do not know. We only know that for a time he was certain he would become a castaway. But we rejoice that in the end he was triumphant.

> Examine yourselves as to whether you are in the faith. Test yourselves. Do you not know yourselves, that Jesus Christ is in you?—unless indeed you are disqualified (2 Corinthians 13:5).

The Greek philosopher Plato said, "The life that is unexamined is not worth living." He was right.

The purpose of self-examination is to be sure that there is veracity and integrity in all we say and do. Our own self-scrutiny is in itself a testimony of the essential value of life and ministry!

Paul recognized that he had "a thorn in the flesh" (2 Corinthians 12:7). We are not sure what it was, but God told him that he would have to put up with it. God also reminded him, "My grace is sufficient for you, for My strength is made perfect in [your] weakness" (v. 9).

The real challenge of self-examination is our basic honesty in dealing with our private discoveries. Some preachers know that what they are doing or how they are behaving is wrong. They seem to feel that since dishonest behavior has become common among secular leadership, the same will be excused in Christian leadership.

Our answer to this error is to point out the tragic cases of public and private dishonesty that have been uncovered by the media. Many public religious figures have become total derelicts because they would not deal honestly with their humanity. We must *constantly* examine ourselves! We must deal with sin if we find it. John said, "If we confess our sins, He is faithful and just to forgive us our sins and to cleanse us from all unrighteousness" (1 John 1:9).

The way of the Cross is not easy. It never will be. Read this when you are overloaded and pressured:

Are they ministers of Christ?—I speak as a fool—I am more: in labors more abundant, in stripes above measure, in prisons more frequently, in deaths often. From the Jews five times I received forty stripes minus one. Three times I was beaten with rods; once I was stoned; three times I was shipwrecked; a night and a day I have been in the deep; in journeys often, in perils of waters, in perils of robbers, in perils of my own countrymen, in perils of the Gentiles, in perils in the city, in perils in the wilderness, in perils in the sea, in perils among false brethren; in weariness and toil, in sleeplessness often, in hunger and thirst, in fastings often, in cold and nakedness—besides the other things, what comes upon me daily: my deep concern for all the churches. Who is weak, and I am not weak? Who is made to stumble, and I do not burn with indignation?

If I boast, I will boast in the things which concern my infirmity. The God and Father of our Lord Jesus Christ, who is blessed forever, knows that I am not lying. In Damascus the governor, under Aretas the king, was guarding the city of the Damascenes with a garrison, desiring to arrest me; but I was let down in a basket through a window in the wall, and escaped from his hands (2 Corinthians 11:23-33).

Let us not sit in spiritual doldrums, feeling sorry for ourselves. We have taken up the most noble calling on earth!

Regardless of how tough it is or how inadequate we may feel, let us glory in the Cross! Let us take up our cross and follow Jesus.

CHAPTER 15

A Tragic Barter of Basic Christian Vision

Christian writer and preacher, W. Graham Scroggie, once said, "If one would be Christ-minded he must be missionary-minded. One who is not has no justification for calling himself a disciple of Christ." *Are you missionary-minded?* As pastors we must never fall into the vision-bartering syndrome of thinking that our parish or local church marks the outer limits of the congregation's Christian responsibility.

Our field is the world! Since Christ is universal, it will take a universe to interpret Him. Our Lord himself said:

"You did not choose Me, but I chose you and appointed you that you should go and bear fruit" (John 15:16).

"As the Father has sent Me, I also send you" (John 20:21).

"Go, therefore and make disciples of all the nations" (Matthew 28:19).

Despite the high level of public and international information provided by the modern media, many Christian leaders have bartered away their world vision. They have adopted, instead, a parochial view that barely sees beyond the nearest street sign.

Too many pastors have developed a "kingdom mentality." They are the king, the church is their castle, and the members are their "subjects." They do not want anyone to interfere with their kingdom or know what is in its treasury.

Hebrews 12:16 calls Esau a "profane person" because he sold the great treasure of his birthright for a mess of pottage. Sadly, God's chosen ministers often become deeply involved with the normal trivia that constantly dogs their steps. As a result, they exchange their international mission vision for a mess of local ecclesiastical pottage.

Local parish issues are important, but they must not rob us of the greatest of all issues, the salvation of a lost world. John Wesley echoed St. Augustine's powerful conviction:

I must have a whole Christ for my salvation,
I must have a whole Bible for my staff,
I must have a whole church for my fellowship,
I must have the whole world for my parish.

Being a visionary is not necessary to have a world vision for Christ, but true missionaries relate to the vision experience of the prophet Isaiah:

> In the year that King Uzziah died, I saw the Lord sitting on a throne, high and lifted up, and the train of His robe filled the temple. Above it stood seraphim; each one had six wings: with two he covered his face, with two he covered his feet, and with two he flew. And one cried to another and said: "Holy, holy, holy is the Lord of hosts; the whole earth is full of His glory!" And the posts of the door were shaken by the voice of him who cried out, and the house was filled with smoke.
>
> So I said: "Woe is me, for I am undone! Because I am a man of unclean lips, and I dwell in the midst of a people of unclean lips; for my eyes have seen the King, the Lord of hosts."
>
> Then one of the seraphim flew to me, having in his hand a live coal which he had taken with the tongs from the altar. And he touched my mouth with it, and said: "Behold, this has touched your lips; your iniquity is taken away, and your sin purged."
>
> Also I heard the voice of the Lord, saying: "Whom shall I send, and who will go for Us?"
>
> Then I said, "Here am I! Send me" (Isaiah 6:1-8).

It is all too clear: (1) the vision of God, (2) the vision of self, and (3) the vision of the world. The missionary enterprise is the heart and life of the church. As one who has pastored in both small and large churches, I know what it is to be so overwhelmed with religious trivia that I felt like the self-disguised prophet who was left in charge of a prisoner taken in battle. He told the king, "While your servant was busy here and there, he was gone" (1 Kings 20:40). I was so busy with unimportant matters that the really important task had been missed.

A church activity calendar can be a pastor's source of condemnation. I have been guilty of writing down such a host of small tasks that the great presentation of the Cross of Christ was left until the last moment or omitted entirely. In my early ministry, a wise Scottish lady said, "We love to hear you talk about the Cross and the saving power of God's grace." She got my attention!

During my study a day or so later, I read Paul's words in Galatians 6:14: "But God forbid that I should boast except in the cross of our Lord Jesus Christ, by whom the world has been crucified to me, and I to the world." Our compassion for the entire lost world must begin with our compassion for our unsaved neighbor across the street, but it must include them both.

In every local church a worldwide mission vision comes from the pulpit. It must be proclaimed from the lips of a man or woman who has struggled mightily to make the congregation and the entire pastoral staff missionary-minded and mission-supporting. I have known of mission efforts in a congregation being stymied by a financial manager who sat stolidly upon his penurious bottom and told his fellow staff members that the congregation could not afford to give to missions. It is not wrong to set aside a special Mission Sunday, but it is wrong if missions is not mentioned as well at every meeting time. This is why the church is in the world.

Missionary apathy is caused by many circumstances, but the chief cause is the lack of vision on the part of Christian leadership. The vision of many pastors is focused on their own congregations and their needs. They feel they do not have time for extensive missionary emphasis. Others simply do not have a missionary vision that reaches beyond their own communities.

There are those, however, who put a great emphasis on missions. Nothing enhances and reinforces this "mission vision" in a congregation more than for some of its own people to go to a mission field. It gives the church a sense of worldwide involvement in the Great Commission.

This encourages sacrificial giving to mission work in foreign lands. When this happens the pastor needs a local missions board or committee to help him administrate the program and keep the mission vision clearly before the people.

Every pastor should be aware of the fact that a

local church missions board can be either a great blessing or a great problem to the church's missionaries. Thus the church should spend some of its missions funds to send one or two missions board members to personally visit their own missionaries on a regular basis. If the missionaries will openly communicate with the visiting board members, missionary outreach will become one of the more rewarding spiritual experiences for the congregation.

When my wife and I were on the field, we had many visits from members of our denominational missions board. It was helpful and supportive. Some missionary friends in other denominations labored brokenheartedly due to "back home" misinterpretations of their work.

Basic cultural ignorance and totally unrealistic concepts on the part of the home missions board make conflict inevitable. It should be obvious, but frequently is not, that home mission work in North America is a far cry from rugged missionary involvement in Africa. There are vast cultural differences, language barriers, primitive conditions, dangerous diseases, not to mention the hazards of travel.

When Merle and I were in Africa, there were no bridges in many places and torrential rains would make the crossing of the river impossible for days at a time! Home missions boards seldom have the remotest idea of what foreign mission labors entail. They must be on the scene from time to time.

The local church missionary departing for the field should not experience a "back door" departure with a small weeknight meeting service. His work is the personal and congregational fulfillment of the Great Commission and should be a stellar event in the life of the congregation.

A parish is a group committed to the pastor by God, for their training and personal involvement in the worldwide task. Therefore, they must recognize that it is through them that God wants to reach the world for Christ.

The missionary board may be committed, but the pastor must diligently lead his flock as a missionary body. No emotional, cultural, scientific or humanistic interest should lead him to barter off his vision of the basic spiritual needs of the world. If that happens, he has no message of importance for the world to hear.

Another point I want to emphasize is that *missionary passion* must never be mistaken for *missionary identification!* Inexperienced and uninformed fervor is often an obstacle to authentic mission work! It lives in the never-never land of unrealistic romanticism. It is as far from the successful fulfillment of the vision as the Congo jungle is from Labrador's Arctic coast.

I know former foreign missionaries whose work was very productive. But due to a total lack of understanding by their supporters back home, they returned to find their work discounted, themselves virtually ignored, and their children so disenchanted that they left home hating anything that had to do with the gospel of Jesus Christ.

May God help us to never let that happen in our home church.

CHAPTER 16

THE PENALTY FOR PULPIT PERJURY

A dictionary defines *perjury* as "voluntary violation of an oath or vow, either by swearing to what is untrue or by omission to do what has been promised under oath." The penalty of perjury, then, is the disadvantage, loss or hardship experienced as a result of false or lying witness or testimony.

The distinguishing feature of genuine Christian preaching and teaching is truth. In John 8:32, Jesus said, "And you shall know the truth, and the truth shall make you free." Before this, He had declared to the Samaritan woman at the well, "God is

Spirit, and those who worship Him must worship in spirit and truth" (4:24).

Truth is the only freedom-producing factor in our lives. Its opposite produces nothing but confusion, uncertainty and enslavement. In a court of law, witnesses are asked to solemnly swear or affirm they will tell the truth, the whole truth and *nothing but the truth.*

The pastor in the pulpit is under no less an obligation. He or she must speak as though testifying before a tribunal of men and observing angels. One of the great temptations Satan places before the preacher is the lure to embellish his stories and illustrations. He is tempted to stray from the factual and add information to make them more interesting or entertaining.

The Christian speaker or teacher can tell the absolute truth in a way that illustrates the point, but does not step over the boundaries of unvarnished fact. The minister may mention that what he will tell is a story he has heard. The listener will then know that it may or may not be true. This may not give it exactly the "punch" one would prefer, but it keeps the minister honest.

A homiletics teacher told our class years ago that those who planned to preach the gospel needed to know the value of good illustrations. I have considered his remarks often. While the words are true, there is another side to the story.

Illustrations are windows that throw light on the facts. However, if those windows are smudged with untruths or exaggeration, they will have a negative effect on both the message and the hearers. This is the opposite of the effect the speaker intends. A half-falsehood is not a half-truth.

The utterance of partial truth is like the story of the shepherd who had three sons who kept a large herd of sheep. They agreed that if one of them saw a wolf approaching, he would cry "Wolf! Wolf!"

One boy decided it would be fun to shout "Wolf! Wolf!" when there was no wolf, just to see the flurry of excitement it caused among his fellow shepherds. It was so much fun the first time that he tried it again . . . and then again. Each time the shepherds ran to his aid only to find that there was no wolf.

His experiment in hilarity backfired when one day a wolf attacked the sheep and when the boy shouted, no one paid any attention to him. As a result, the predator destroyed many sheep before help finally arrived.

Half-truths must be looked upon as lies. They are poisonous and just as destructive as the unadulterated lie. There is no such thing as what some people call "little white lies"—if white is to represent purity and truth

Sermon-destroying falsehoods have a gradually abrasive effect on the credibility of preaching. They eventually discolor the declaration of what would otherwise be pure Biblical truth.

Utterances that are obviously unlikely to be true become fiction in the minds of hearers who will then question the veracity of anything we say. As messengers of truth we cannot afford to take this risk. No man of God can tell lies and think he will get away with it. "Be sure your sin will find you out" (Numbers 32:23).

If we cannot rely on the veracity of our recall in the illustrations we use, many will discern the liberties we are taking. When our illustrations attempt to describe the attitudes and actions of other people, *we must tell the truth.* Personal integrity suffers every time the audience discerns fictional statements that are not identified as such.

No man or woman of God can play games with the truth. Every preacher who wishes to be known as a "man of God" must remember that he will never earn that title unless he is first "a man of truth."

I once overheard students at a Bible school where I was president, arguing vigorously about remarks made in chapel by a visiting speaker. He had used illustrations that were, without doubt, questionable. One remarked, "I don't care if he has a reputation as a Christian leader. I believe that if he will stretch the truth about one thing, he will do it with other things, too!"

Obviously, the man was trying to impress the students. He did, but not in the way he intended. His practice of distorting and misrepresenting the truth became the topic of discussion for a long time and he was never asked to return.

Once a preacher builds a reputation for falsehood or perjury in the pulpit, whether he realizes it or not, he has damaged himself almost beyond repair. Not even a public apology will persuade his listeners that his word can be trusted.

In the Sermon on the Mount, Jesus said, "But let your 'Yes' be 'Yes,' and your 'No,' 'No.' For whatever is more than these is from the evil one" (Matthew 5:37). As speakers for God, our words are the only means of communication we have. What we say should be as simple as "Yes" or "No!" Anything beyond this comes from evil.

The saddest thing about this kind of exaggeration is that it becomes an insidious habit in both public and private utterance. What some speakers call "adding a little spice to the story" is actually adding untruth to an otherwise honest statement. Untruths and exaggeration are like poison: it doesn't take much to destroy good food or listener confidence.

Since *unadulterated* truth sets people free, the opposite chains them and prevents the liberating power of the gospel from being heard and understood. As God's men and women, we will be graded by our skill in using words to draw humankind to

Christ. Proverbs 25:11 declares, "A word fitly spoken is like apples of gold in settings of silver." Jesus uttered the most powerful passage in the New Testament on the importance of spoken words:

> "Either make the tree good and its fruit good, or else make the tree bad and its fruit bad; for a tree is known by its fruit. Brood of vipers! How can you, being evil, speak good things? For out of the abundance of the heart the mouth speaks. A good man out of the good treasure of his heart brings forth good things, and an evil man out of the evil treasure brings forth evil things. But I say to you that for every idle word men may speak, they will give account of it in the day of judgment. For by your words you will be justified, and by your words you will be condemned" (Matthew 12:33-37).

The secrets of our inner selves usually leak out through our mouths! Wholesome speaking comes from wholesome thinking. This was Christ's primary point when He said, "How can you, being evil, speak good things?" (v. 34). There is no such thing as disciplined speaking without first having mastered disciplined thinking.

Proverbs 23:7 confirms this: "For as he thinks in his heart, so is he." Regardless of how careful the careless thinker may be, sooner or later he or she will unwittingly proclaim his or her true inner self, "for out of the abundance of the heart the mouth speaks" (Matthew 12:34).

Verse 36 is the real clincher for us. Jesus continued to develop His remarks about careless and risque talk: "Every idle word men may speak, they will give account of it in the day of judgment." In the original text, the revealing word for "idle" is the Greek *argon.* It means "lazy, useless, careless or debasing."

As we attempt to use words of truth to proclaim God's message, we need to shop carefully for terms that accurately proclaim genuine integrity and un-adulterated truth! This is powerfully stated in Jesus' words: "By your words you will be justified, and by your words you will be condemned" (v. 37).

Moments of unguarded dialogue in communion with others often become the undoing of some self-proclaimed "holy thinkers." In ordinary conversation outside the pulpit or study, men and women of God often let down their guards and permit a spiritually debased mind to surface in their spoken communications.

A young pastor once remarked to me, "When I get with the guys, I speak like the guys because I don't want them to be uncomfortable at all in my presence." He had forgotten what Paul said in Philippians 4:8:

> Finally, brethren, whatever things are true, whatever things are noble, whatever things are just, whatever things are pure, whatever things are lovely, whatever things are of good report, if there is any virtue and if there is anything praiseworthy—meditate on these things.

The servant of God, whether with the "guys" or someone else, must remember Colossians 4:6:

Let your speech always be with grace, seasoned
with salt, that you may know how you ought to answer each one.

The only way to reach men and women is to
speak straightforwardly with integrity and truthfulness, so that the convicting power of the Holy
Spirit can move them through your words.

CHAPTER 17

THE SACREDNESS OF HOLY THINGS AND SEASONS

*O*ne of the most common problems faced by God's men and women in ministry to-day, and one which must be guarded against prayerfully and carefully, is a unique combination of hidden pride and spiritual insensitivity. I refer to an almost imperceptible encroachment of routine work upon our observance of holy things.

I was awed the first time I officiated at Holy Communion. It was so new to me and, I admit, a bit frightening. I had always loved to attend Communion services because of the deep meaning of the elements, the wine and the bread. However, after many Communion services I found myself becoming insensitive to the sacredness of the Eucharist. It was something we did on the first Sunday of every month, another feature of programming which meant one or two hymns must be omitted from the regular service to leave room.

As I prepared my part in this observance one Sunday, I remembered a time in Malawi (then called *Nyasaland*) when I was holding a pastor's seminar. Primitive African pastors sat before me on the bare ground inside a thorn *boma*. Some of them had never been in a Communion service. I gave a play-by-play summary of the events of the day of Christ's crucifixion, wanting to associate His death with the meaning of the elements.

As I told the story, I saw great sorrow come into the eyes of my listeners. They had never heard it in such detail. When I came to the moment of our Lord's death, some of them were weeping in deep despair! I realized I must move quickly to the triumph of Christ's resurrection.

I related the appearance of the angel sitting on the stone at the tomb's entrance. When I described the angel's words proclaiming "He is not here, He is risen!" the listeners leaped from their places, shouting and dancing in exultant worship!

At that moment I first realized the true meaning of Holy Communion. It is a celebration of Resurrection victory, for His death without His resurrection would have been meaningless, and a terrible finale!

Another fact that makes Communion special is that it is a testimony of faith in the second coming of Jesus. In 1 Corinthians 11:26, the apostle Paul declared, "For as often as you eat this bread and drink this cup, you proclaim the Lord's death till He comes."

I shall never forget the fervent prayer from the lips of a woman in her 90s as she took Communion. Tears were running down her wrinkled cheeks as she took the chalice in her trembling hands. She prayed, "O my Father, You have been so good to me all of these years. I am now drinking this cup, hoping that Jesus will come before I return here to take it again. I am waiting and looking for You to come any day!"

Her wish should be the wish of every true believer in the Lord Jesus. That godly, ancient handmaiden of the Lord moved my heart and caused me to look more earnestly and impatiently for His returning.

Recently I came to 2 Chronicles 26 in my devotional reading. It is the moving story of the life of one of Judah's greatest kings, Uzziah. His contemporaries and counselors were the prophets Isaiah and Zechariah. From the day he was crowned at age 16, King Uzziah feared God. His reign was a tremendous success in every way. His armies subjugated his enemies. Prosperity came to the land and its people. He built great fortifications and new cities, and trade flourished throughout Palestine. He personally sought the will of God and was given the spiritual understanding of many mysteries. He appeared to be God's ideal servant-king, and the things of God were holy to him.

Then a tragic series of events occurred, causing Uzziah's spiritual sensitivity to wane. A spirit of pride grew in him. He who had been so faithful in observing the laws of sacrifice and worship allowed those very things to become routine. Ultimately, he decided he did not need the ministry of God's appointed priests; he himself would burn incense on the altar of incense. This rite, according to the Law, was the sole privilege of the priesthood. Leprosy broke out on his forehead, and the priests had to remove him from the Holy Place. That mighty king died a horrible death as a leper.

What a sobering lesson for all who serve as leaders of God's people, and who permit the holy awe of sacred things to disappear from their minds. This lesson applies equally to water baptism, the observance of Christmas and Easter, and the dedication of little children to God. We must never allow ourselves to lose our sense of the sacredness of these holy occasions.

Baptism is the outward sign of the mighty inward fact of regeneration. The baptism of Jesus was not the last time God spoke to people at a baptismal service. Frequently during our years in African mission work, I was reminded in powerful ways of the importance of water baptism in the eyes of both believers and unbelievers.

In the United States, some churches have baptismal services on weeknights or Sunday afternoons, instead of during the regular services.

Consequently, many parishioners and their families do not think it merits much attention, or that it is even a bona fide part of the Christian faith.

In Africa, we always baptized in rivers or lakes. Frequently the crowds of pagan onlookers on the opposite river bank would be at least three times as large as that of the Christian believers on my side. One day I asked one of my African pastors, "Why is this?" He replied, "Oh, those people across the river know that when one of their friends is baptized, he has left forever his old way of living, speaking and thinking. They have come to say 'goodbye' to him. They know that when baptized believers come up out of that water, they are new people."

How I wish all baptized people left the same impression on their unsaved friends and relatives! This is why water baptism is called an outward sign of an inward work of the Holy Spirit.

We must emphasize to family and friends—and anyone who will stop and listen—the sacredness of Christmas, Easter, the baptism of a friend, or the glorious rebirth of one who has just found Christ as Lord and Master. Every believer should rejoice with other believers as we watch the Eastern skies for His lightning-like arrival with the scepter of eternity in His hand.

We should ignore the pagan commercialization of Christmas and take our human sheep back to the manger in Bethlehem. We should gaze once more into the face of the Christ child.

At Easter, let us forget the Easter eggs and rabbits, and accompany the women to the open tomb. Let us hear once more the angel's announcement, "He is not here, He has risen!"

When we dedicate a baby, let us remember the unseen promises of tomorrow for that child. He or she may become another servant of Christ like Billy Graham, David Livingstone or Dwight L. Moody. This child may, indeed, be called to a God-called ministry that will eclipse anything we will ever do for God.

You must never permit the awe of sacred and holy things and seasons to diminish. Find ways to keep them as fresh and alive as when you first experienced them, so you can pass that excitement and wonder on to your people.

CHAPTER 18

MAINTAINING BASIC CHRISTIANITY

*I*n our rapidly changing society, every formerly established concept is being challenged. Many of these challenges are being proclaimed by people who speak of a "new world order." The truth is that they do not understand the values and principles that governed the "old world order" against which they are protesting.

The message seems to imply, "If it's new it has to be better than the old." As a result, we have seen an increase over the past 40 years in every kind of lawlessness known to humanity. The wholesale destruction of life through warfare, murder, suicide and abortion captures the news headlines every evening. This doesn't include the effect on the inner man—an impact which raises the stress level to that of a mental pressure cooker.

Many are so obsessed with the idea of this mythical new order that they have never bothered to find out what the old order consisted of. While trying to construct a kind of utopian society, they seem unaware that they are destroying the basic building blocks of any social order, new or old. The *home* and *family* are crucial building blocks that are gradually being eliminated.

In the twilight of the greatest society in human history, where does the church find a reason for existence? Have we become irrelevant as some have declared? A friend said recently that Christianity seems to be stumbling and faltering. "What kind of Christianity do you mean?" I asked him. "Are you talking about historic, eternally relevant Christianity, or of the varieties of entertaining 'religious activity' that parade under the banner of Christianity?"

Secular entertainers always have a wider field in which to operate than religious leaders do. This seems to have led many pastors and evangelists to move toward entertainment to attract a large congregation. But the more sensational we appear to be, the less believable we are to the searching minds and hearts of people. G.K. Chesterton once said, "The greatest problem with Christianity is not that it has been tried and found wanting, but that it has hardly been tried at all."

When Jesus commissioned the first Christian messengers, He gave them instructions to heal the sick, cleanse the lepers, raise the dead and cast out demons. He said He came to bind up the brokenhearted and set free those who were bound. Then He added, "As the Father has sent Me, I also send you" (John 20:21).

Many Christian leaders forget that they minister to masses of confused, hurting, lonely and guilt-ridden people who seek forgiveness and soul peace. Sensationalism may get the crowd's attention, but it sends them home empty and unsatisfied. Hurting people want deliverance from pain. Heartbroken people need inner healing. Guilt-ridden people need forgiveness.

One pastor remarked that he seemed to be serving a transient congregation. "They are nothing more than a 'coming and going' crowd," he complained. Some communities do have transient workers who are unable to maintain regular church attendance. But I could not help but wonder if this man's congregation had become a mixture of religious attendees looking for a place to be fed, healed, comforted and forgiven.

Sheep looking for better pastures simply wander from place to place in search of a sheepfold where they will be sheltered, fed and have their wounds dressed and healed. The basic question that we as God's under-shepherds must ask is, "What am I trying to provide for my people?"

Are we primarily seeking to supply a pleasant, entertaining church atmosphere? Or are we trying to challenge unscriptural lifestyles and beliefs, and lead them people into a deeper relationship with God? The Lord's basic purpose in developing Christianity was, first of all, to bring about a new relationship through which humans could associate with the Creator! Are we as pastors focused on God's purpose? Or are we really focused on improving man's relationship with man?

Any program that is sociologically comforting to troubled people will become popular, even if there is nothing Christian about it. If it encourages a benign but Christless lifestyle, it will become a comfortable religion. Genuine New Testament Christianity, however, confronts sinners with their own unregenerated status. Each person must be brought face-to-face with an all-knowing righteous God who wishes to transform man so that He can fellowship with him in a loving Creator/creature relationship forever.

The Holy Scriptures picture man exactly as his inner conscience assesses him. When he comes face-to-face with God, man has an inherent sense of right and wrong. At that moment he becomes conscious of his own sinfulness and of God's sinlessness. Undiluted Biblical, nonjudgmental gospel preaching confirms man's sinfulness. It also tells him how to become reconciled to God. The solution of this sin question should be the basic motivation for the non-Christian. It is simply to listen to the gospel of Christ until he has been reconciled to God through faith in Jesus' redemptive work on his behalf.

When the message and ministry of the church does not identify a sinner's lost estate and bring him under conviction for his sinfulness, it fails in its mission in the world. Man is an emotional, social creature, and he responds positively to a pleasant social atmosphere. If the church adds the spiritual anesthesia of unscriptural but exciting entertainment to this setting, there will never be a sense of sin in those who attend.

Genuine gospel preaching develops an atmosphere of spiritual conviction. Where the gospel is not proclaimed, moral and ethically minded sinners are undisturbed. They happily involve themselves in religious activities that aren't really Christian. These people are legion throughout Christianity. We must bring them face-to-face with the real message of Christ's cross!

Spiritual leaders must remember Peter's words that "all should come to repentance" (2 Peter 3:9). Jesus said, "Most assuredly, I say to you, unless one is born again, he cannot see the kingdom of God" (John 3:3). Verse 5 repeats the warning.

Maintaining basic and pure Christianity involves more than maintaining a congregation. There are many large congregations which, in the Scriptural sense, are really not "churches." They are but large, exciting religious/social clubs. The questions of sin, repentance and redemption are never discussed in their teaching or preaching. Consequently, those who gather in their assemblies have no Biblical answer for the haunting inner consciousness of sin and failure that dogs their consciences. The task of the church is clear:

> Now all things are of God, who has reconciled us to Himself through Jesus Christ, and has given us the ministry of reconciliation, that is, that God was in Christ reconciling the world to Himself, not imputing their trespasses to them, and has committed to us the word of reconciliation. Now then, we are ambassadors for Christ, as though God were pleading through us: we implore you on Christ's behalf, be reconciled to God (2 Corinthians 5:18-20).

As long as a church ministers genuine Christianity to lost and hurting souls, it will always be relevant. Hospitals that deal with bodily pain and suffering are growing in numbers and importance in all the countries of the world. We have a basic mission in the world. As long as we maintain that mission, we, too, will be relevant.

Let us covenant to carry out Christ's basic assignment to us by healing the brokenhearted, ministering to the heavy-laden and bringing them into His rest.

CHAPTER 19

Dangers That Lurk on the Alternate Road

*A*lternatives for the genuine are growing at an alarming rate. Grocery shoppers learn the trade names of hundreds of substitute foods, some good and many not so good. Generally, substitutes are cheaper to make and some supply dietary needs for a shorter period of time than do the originals. For some time-margarine has taken the place of butter, and only recently has science decided that in many cases, butter is more healthful than some brands of margarine.

An alternate route is taken by some in the pulpit. Some ministers try to find more palatable approaches to the Word of God. Their aim is to soften its righteous demands on the followers of Christ. Terms for *sin* in general—*immorality, dishonesty* and *evil*—have been softened by the use of more tolerable synonyms.

The first sign of this deceptive route is seen when the man or woman of God becomes regretful, fearful or apologetic in regard to clear-cut Biblical demands. Instead of calling for straightforward confession and repentance, the preacher calls for "moral renewal" and "enlightened reflection" on human behavior.

Everyone knows if he or she has sinned; why not proclaim it openly and factually? When we become ill with some kind of contagion, we insist on being told the absolute truth about the nature of the illness and the possibility of regaining our health. The sins of alcoholism and drug abuse, for instance, are deadly in their long-term effects. They destroy the mental and bodily health of those trapped by them. Medical science struggles to cope with these twin evils that destroy thousands of lives every year. Yet, we don't refer to them as minor issues.

Why, then, should God's servants use alternative terms to define and identify sin and wickedness?

One of my secretaries was a victim of this kind of alternative diagnosis. She had the beginnings of breast cancer, but her doctor told her that they were "benign growths." The tragedy was that my secretary took the doctor at her word without getting a second opinion. A few months later the cancer reached the incurable stage and ultimately took her life. Her husband and friends lost her to that deadly disease because of an innocuous, but erroneous, diagnosis.

Do we as ministers of truth dare give a comfortable, but fatal, diagnosis of sin and evil? What causes servants of God to choose a substitute for truth in proclaiming the gospel? It goes back to the basic error of one's personal interpretation of Jesus. How do you present Him? Jesus said, "And I, if I am lifted up from the earth, will draw all people to Myself" (John 12:32).

He was the Prince of teachers. He was the Great Example and the Purest of the Pure. But He was far more! We dabble in trivialities when we refer to Jesus as "the Great Example," "the Ideal Man," "the Prophet of Truth," and so forth. These terms emphasize His humanity without declaring His deity. The angel announcing His birth declared, "You shall call His name Jesus, for He will save His people from their sins" (Matthew 1:21).

To say that the purpose of His coming was only to provide us with a glowing example is to deny everything for which He came. His God-ordained reason for coming to earth was to be a *sacrifice* for our sins. His gift was not just a beautiful lesson in veracity and morality; He came that we might have spiritual life—eternally and abundantly. Paul declared, "Christ died for our sins according to the Scriptures" (1 Corinthians 15:3).

When we preach ethical attainment as the gospel instead of God's plan through Christ's death and resurrection, we attempt to provide a substitute for Jesus the Savior. Any other presentation of Him encourages religious profession without repentance and spiritual transformation, and Christless hypocrisy.

Remember, a hypocrite is one who keeps up a show of professed attainment that he has never reached because of a lack of the divine dimension of grace.

I do not imply that change is wrong. I served on a pastoral staff where change took place, but not at the expense of truth and the gospel. New programs were designed to help people understand the gospel more easily. Others encouraged them to be more active in presenting the gospel to the unchurched. Still others encouraged people to become involved in the ministries of the church.

These kinds of changes are simply improved methods of making the church effective and the gospel understandable. No change that softens the gospel appeal and the Holy Spirit's conviction should ever be considered. Old-fashioned repentance is never out-of-date. We must remind seekers that *all* are sinners and true repentance is the Biblical way of acknowledging human sinfulness and finding God's forgiveness!

I once counseled a woman who was greatly distraught and guilt-ridden. The sins of her past were bad, but they were not uncommon. From the gospel's standpoint, they were certainly forgivable! I told her that I was not her confessor but that God wanted to help her. Our conversation went something like this:

"Pastor, I'm really ashamed to tell you my sins. I knew when I committed them that they were evil and against everything I know of God and His Son, Jesus Christ." "Why, then, did you come to me?" I asked. "Well," she said, "You are a human being, and you know what temptation is."

I turned to Hebrews 4:15 and read to her, "We do not have a High Priest who cannot sympathize with our weaknesses, but was in all points tempted as we are, yet without sin."

"Jesus did not fall to those temptations, but He understands where you have failed," I reminded her. I didn't water down the fact of her sinful behavior, but encouraged her to seek God's forgiveness, since Scripture clearly states that He understands. I prayed aloud in her presence that she would have the courage to acknowledge her sins to God in the name of Jesus, her Savior.

Quietly, she began to weep and then ask God's forgiveness for her sin. She apologized for letting her parents down and asked God's help in avoiding sin in the future. After a few minutes of quiet weeping and prayer, she looked into my face and said, "Pastor, I feel so clean inside! I believe I have become a Christian; I know God has forgiven me!"

That was a triumphant moment for me! It taught me a few more facts about how to lead people to faith and forgiveness at the foot of the Cross. I recount this to remind us that the gospel of Christ and the sinfulness of humanity have not changed. Neither has the simplicity of the gospel! We don't need an alternative to make it effective. Paul warns against crafty psychological maneuvering in order to make converts:

> We should no longer be children, tossed to and fro and carried about with every wind of doctrine, by the trickery of men, in the cunning craftiness of deceitful plotting, but, speaking the truth in love, may grow up in all things into Him who is the head—Christ (Ephesians 4:14, 15).

The truths of God's Word don't need to be psychologically restated in order to lead people into saving grace and spiritual deliverance. This alternate route is nothing less than what Paul called it—"trickery and craftiness." It is a denial of the power of the gospel to change people's lives.

Every honest person I've ministered to is aware that he has sinned. Most want to be forgiven and receive inner strength to help them avoid sin in the future. The redeeming power of the gospel can be presented without condemnation to those who want to believe and repent.

CHAPTER 20

Are You Living at Wits' End Corner?

*T*he most experienced of God's children sometimes reach a point of desperation. They pray
all the prayers they can think of, use all the
wisdom and prudence they possess, and take
counsel from their best advisers; still, the situation seemingly becomes more hopeless. They come
to "wits' end corner" in their Christian lives.

In our devotions, my wife, Merle, and I came
upon this moving passage:

> Those who go down to the sea in ships, who do
> business on great waters, they see the works of
> the Lord, and His wonders in the deep. For He
> commands and raises the stormy wind, which lifts

up the waves of the sea. They mount up to the heavens, they go down again to the depths; their soul melts because of trouble. They reel to and fro, and stagger like a drunken man, and are at their wits' end.

Then they cry out to the Lord in their trouble, and He brings them out of their distresses. He calms the storm, so that its waves are still. Then they are glad because they are quiet; so He guides them to their desired haven. Oh, that men would give thanks to the Lord for His goodness, and for His wonderful works to the children of men! (Psalm 107:23-31).

The man obviously had experience with merchant ships. He knew what it was like to ride out a storm, and to come to wits' end corner before deliverance got there. Speaking of those who did business in great waters, he described their despair on the heaving deck of a ship in a tempest. Verse 27 reminded me of times in my life when I had come to my wits' end. Looking back, I discovered why I found myself in that predicament:

- The entire voyage had been something of *my own doing.* I had not prayed about it before embarking. From the beginning I had doubts about its outcome.

- I had put *too much trust in my own judgment,* and had not sought God's direction.

- I had obtained *counsel from unspiritual men* whose secular ideas had brought me to this unhappy conclusion.

- A few times it was the result of the devious schemes of unprincipled men whom I had trusted and who had deliberately misled me.

- Eventually I came to the conclusion that God himself had permitted me to land at wits' end corner to remind me that without Him I could do nothing.

Once I told a valued mentor I had reached the end of my rope and he said, "Very well. Tie a knot in it and hang on until God arrives." I never forgot that advice. When the people had done everything they knew to ride out the storm, "they [cried] out to the Lord in their trouble" (v. 28). How like us! We do not call on God seriously until we have come to the end of our own efforts. This isn't a sin; it is simply trusting in ourselves until the last desperate minute before we do the right thing. If we would learn to call on God earlier, we would experience the deliverance and calm earlier as well!

When we come to our own wits' end corner, and the sea of life is showing its teeth and threatening to destroy us, there is something we must do. We must trust God and call on Him. Then we must obey what He tells us to do! If we don't do our part in true worship, obedience, confession and repentance, we need not expect Him to lift us out of our predicament.

Sir Humphrey Gilbert, the great ship captain

who founded the first English-speaking colony in North America, brought immigrants to the New World on trans-Atlantic voyages.

On one memorable trip, his great sailing ship encountered a hurricane off the coast of the Azores. The crew struck the sail and dropped an anchor to keep the bow of the ship facing into the storm. Mighty oak timbers creaked and groaned as the ship was pounded by the waves. Everyone ran below to escape the fury of the tempest. As time passed, the crew members noticed that their godly captain was missing.

Finally, the first mate went above to look for him on deck. Seeing a light in the helmsman's cabin, he struggled across the slippery deck and opened the door. The captain was sitting on a stool beside the helm, calmly reading his Bible. As he closed the door and stood before Sir Humphrey, the first mate cried: "Thank God you are safe, Captain! But what about the ship?"

Sir Humphrey asked, "Have we done all we can to secure her against the storm?"

"Yes sir!" answered the first mate.

"Well," said the Captain, "We must trust God, my friend, because heaven is as near by water as it is by land!"

Remember this when you come to your own wits' end corner. When troubles assail individuals or the church as a whole, the pastor has an excellent opportunity to provide encouraging leadership.

Paul gave comfort and encouragement to others in desperate situations. He is the example of a true leader as he shows us how to face discouraging circumstances. "Three times I was shipwrecked; a night and a day I have been in the deep," he wrote in 2 Corinthians 11:25. We do not know exactly when this happened during his dangerous and colorful career. But we do know what he did during the shipwreck on his voyage to Rome (see Acts 27:20-44).

The ship Paul sailed on had been in the midst of a violent storm for several days. Finally, God spoke to him, assuring him that everyone on board would be saved. Because there was an aura of truth and power in his words, his bearing and his commands, even the ship's crew obeyed Paul's instructions. They, and Paul, fortified themselves with food.

After throwing the ship's tackle and the balance of the cargo of valuable wheat into the sea, they ran the ship aground on one of Malta's beaches. They continued to follow Paul's instructions until at last they "escaped safely to land."

The 276 people aboard all trusted Paul's leadership. His authoritative actions teach us that people in distress seek strong and definitive leadership. Thus, wits' end corner is a place of spiritual opportunity. In every Christian service there are both believers and unbelievers who struggle in their own dilemmas.

Like the frightened sailors on Paul's ill-fated ship, we are looking for genuine leadership. God's Word has answers if we will take time to look for them. Once we know these answers, we can proclaim them with power and authority.

Those who do not search for answers in the Word of God never experience the peace of God through Christ. As Christian leaders we must be sensitive to the fact that many parishioners, as well as unregenerate friends who come to church with them, are "at sea" with a storm raging in their hearts. Their faces may not reflect their trauma, but it is there nontheless.

Early in my ministry I did not fully realize this. After I began counseling, I discovered that untroubled facial expressions are often a deliberate camouflage to prevent others from discovering the tempest tearing people apart. We must specialize in counseling and comforting God's people.

A Christian lady whom I considered to be stable and unruffled said to me one day, "My attendance at church here is the most wonderful time of my week. I find peace, encouraging words, and true spiritual worship and fellowship in this sanctuary. I can leave my troubles and fears right here!"

It never appeared to me that she had any serious troubles, and she did not reveal them. But this short conversation reminded me that wonderful things were happening in God's house. We are

totally unaware of many of the things God is doing in His house when we minister faithfully. This
is always the case.

Many Christians are unquestional by vocal about
their troubles, but a larger percentage do not share
their problems with anyone but God. They often
make undesignated requests for prayer because
they know God is fully acquainted with the details of their situation.

I recall the encouraging remarks a husband and
wife in one of our more stalwart families made to
me one day. Both expressed their deep gratitude
for the ministry they were receiving at the church.
Yet, they did not name the specific areas of blessing.

They simply said to me: "Pastor, you have no
idea how you have been discerning our problems and addresing them in your preaching. We
know God has been leading you in many remarks
you have made. You spelled out our problems
exactly and taught us how to handle them."

To this day I have no idea exactly what their
problems were. But as always, the loving and clear
presentation of God's Word ministered to them.
When presented in the proper way, the Word of
God will minister to many in your congregation
whom you do not know are gratefully receiving
them! You can cast your bread upon the waters
and it will do its mighty work, coming back to you in

unrecognized blessings and in the lives of those to whom you lovingly minister.

Let us remain faithful in sowing the seeds and watering the soil of human hearts. Then we must leave the harvest, which we may never see personally, to the eyes and pleasure of the living God.

CHAPTER 21

SELF-EXAMINATION, THE SUPREME TEST

I would be remiss if I did not challenge you, my ministerial colleagues, to personally follow one of the most difficult exercises commanded by the Holy Scriptures. That exercise is the Biblical exhortation to painstakingly and privately examine oneself in the presence of God. This intimate activity is based on our private, personal relationship with God. King David prayed:

> Search me, O God, and know my heart; try me, and know my anxieties; and see if there is any wicked way in me, and lead me in the way everlasting (Psalm 139:23, 24).

In 2 Corinthians 13:5, the apostle Paul instructed

believers, "Examine yourselves as to whether you are in the faith. Test yourselves. Do you not know yourselves, that Jesus Christ is in you?—unless indeed you are disqualified." These facts encourage us in a powerful way to undertake self-examination on a regular basis:

God, through His Word, commands us to examine ourselves, but our obedience to His command is purely volitional on our part.

Sermons by our friends may encourage us to examine ourselves, but we must initiate the action.

Other believers may sense our need for self-examination, but they are usually reluctant to encourage us to do so.

The Holy Spirit often directs us to get alone with God in genuine soul-searching privacy, but the first step in that direction must be a decisive reaction on our part in response to His leading.

In searching the Scriptures during sermon preparation, I have sensed my need for privacy and self-examination before God. Often I put off an immediate response with the excuse that my schedule forces me to postpone it. But Satan can use my scheduled moments as excuses to avoid attending to immediate spiritual needs. During a class in pastoral theology, our teacher reminded us that there were three absolute essentials in entering Christian ministry:

- Seek to know God personally and intimately.

- Strive to know and understand humanity.

Fellow men and women are the focus of my ministry and service.

- Strive to know myself as people see me, as God sees me and as I know myself to be.

I have found that I am frequently unhappy with myself when I consider what others, and God, see in me. God knows me intimately whether I understand Him or not. But how do the sheep to whom I minister see me? How am I coming across to them? In my years of service to God, I have discovered that the closer I walk to God and the more intimate I am with Him, the better my sheep think of me and love me.

In my early ministry I struggled to be what I thought others wanted me to be. This was a great mistake. A seminary teacher was asked, "How will I be able to create the right impression in the eyes of my parishioners?" The teacher responded, "Take care of your character and relationship with God, and God will take care of your reputation and the impression you make."

Periodic, honest self-scrutiny in the presence of God, while often painful, is by far the most effective way of fulfilling our holy calling. To really know humanity, I must see people as God sees them and as He defines their condition. When we are truly alone with God, we see lost humanity in true spiritual soul passion and reality.

Solitary self-analysis in the sight of God enables us to be real in the sight of our people. The holier-than-thou preacher will soon have a small audience of parishioners, but the servant of God who sees himself clearly as a "sinner," but saved by grace, will quickly identify with the people. Our relationship with God can influence sinful humanity only when we see our own sinfulness in the sight of God.

Self-examination is the shortest road to this life-changing revelation. One of the painful advantages of spending time with God in private is that nothing is hidden from Him. Communication with God is always on an as-it-is-right-now basis. Our past cannot be changed, and God is not interested in it. Our future is the part of eternal life we have not yet experienced.

In John 10:27, 28, Jesus said, "My sheep hear My voice, and I know them, and they follow Me. And I give them eternal life, and they shall never perish; neither shall anyone snatch them out of My hand." In this scripture the word *give* is from the Greek *didomi*, which is the present tense. He did not say, "I *will* give," but "I now give." Eternal life begins when we become a child of God. The best way for us to know Jesus Christ is in deep self-reflection before Him on a daily basis in prayer and communion.

Years ago a student asked me, "How do I achieve effective self-examination in the presence of the

Lord?" I reminded him that Jesus said if one wishes to be a servant of God, he or she must be willing to trust the leading of the Holy Spirit.

"When He, the Spirit of truth, has come, He will guide you into all truth; for He will not speak on His own authority, but whatever He hears He will speak; and He will tell you things to come" (John 16:13).

It is impossible to have intimate communion with God the Father and God the Son without first having intimate communion with the Holy Spirit. Attending to the voice of the Holy Spirit is the first requirement. Long before we get alone with the Lord Jesus, the Spirit has been dealing with things in our lives that need attention. When we do get alone with Christ, those are the first things He will bring up.

At times my godly wife sees things in my life she feels I should deal with. I am often secretly aware of them but have postponed addressing them. It is uncomfortable when a marriage companion is moved by the Holy Spirit to encourage the spouse to examine his or her behavior. Those with genuine marriage companionship and unity know what I am talking about.

Christians who have been alone with God in penitence and tears know that it is not an experience of self-exaltation and ecstasy. Finding oneself in the presence of God where pretense and make-believe are banished by heart-searching truth is almost always painful. If we, as pastoral shepherds and leaders, do not attend to this very crucial exercise, how can we encourage our fellow Christians to do so?

Now we come to an almost equally important action in respect to our self-examination in God's presence. We cannot spend time in His presence without resolving the wounds inflicted on us.

As we examine past and present relationships which God brings to light, we find that there are issues we must face and correct. We often try to forget many things without making confession and seeking forgiveness of the injured party.

Some secret sins, however, are better left secret if they are in the sea of God's forgetfulness. We have enough to handle if we deal with those sins and errors others know about. A member of another parish once said to me, "Our pastor says he has been alone with God. I will believe it when I see some changes in him."

If we spend real time with God, we will be more like Him. We must not be afraid of the awe-inspiring presence of God. He has asked us to fellowship with Him, and we will always find Him waiting if we make spending time with Him a priority.

The terrible reality is that if we do not meet with God privately and examine ourselves under His unwavering gaze, we will be obliged to walk alone in a dark and lonely world.

CHAPTER 22

DEALING WITH QUESTIONS OF HOLINESS AND SIN

*H*oliness of heart and mind as a divine requirement of believers in God is not emphasized as it was when I became a Christian, but it is a matter of prime importance to the person called to pastoral ministry. The central history of both the Old and New Testaments tells of God's dealings with the sinfulness of fallen humanity. Numerous Old Testament passages reveal God's laws for sacrifices for sin.

The central theme of the New Testament is God's redemptive work through His Son's vicarious death for sinful humanity. Christ's death on the Cross ended the Old Testament sacrificial system, and His sacrifice purchased full redemption from sin for all who accept Him as Lord.

What is sin? *Sin is a lack of conformity to the character, nature and will of God, whether that lack is in act, disposition, state, thought or will.* This does not, however, abolish the power and reality of sin for those who have accepted Him and experienced the new birth. We became new creatures in Christ the moment we accepted Him as Savior.

We soon discovered, however, that we still had to deal with the temptation, wrong thinking, unguarded speech and other issues that are nothing short of sin. We were sure that we were new creatures because the new birth wrought a tremendous change in us. Where did these new powerful temptations come from?

For what I am doing, I do not understand. For what I will to do, that I do not practice; but what I hate, that I do. If, then, I do what I will not to do, I agree with the law that it is good. But now, it is no longer I who do it, but sin that dwells in me. For I know that in me (that is, in my flesh) nothing good dwells; for to will is present with me but how to perform what is good I do not find. For the good that I will to do, I do not do; but the evil I will not to do, that I practice. Now if I do what I will not to do, it is no longer I who do it, but sin that dwells in me.

I find then a law, that evil is present with me, the one who wills to do good. For I delight in the law of God according to the inward man. But I see another law in my members, warring against the law of my mind, and bringing me into captivity to the law of sin which is in my members. O wretched man that I am! Who will deliver me from this body of death? I thank God—through Jesus Christ our Lord!

So then, with the mind I myself serve the law of God, but with the flesh the law of sin (Romans 7:15-25).

When I was young in Christianity, I met a few preachers who taught sinless perfection. They declared that this passage was speaking of religious sinners trying to live for Christ without being converted. To the contrary, it clearly addresses the experience of the born-again Christian who tries to live a Christian life in his or her own strength. No sinner "delights in the law of God" in his inner man. Here is Paul's description of the unregenerate man:

As it is written: "There is none righteous, no, not one; there is none who understands; there is none who seeks after God. They have all turned aside; they have together become unprofitable; there is none who does good, no, not one."

"Their throat is an open tomb; with their tongues they have practiced deceit";

"The poison of asps is under their lips";

"Whose mouth is full of cursing and bitterness."

"Their feet are swift to shed blood; destruction and misery are in their ways; and the way of peace they have not known."

"There is no fear of God before their eyes" (Romans 3:10-18).

Such is the Biblical picture of the inward and outward life of the unregenerate person. Godless people choose not to reveal their inward wickedness for the sake of their own code of behavior. During the 20th century, however, man's inhumanity toward his own kind was graphically demonstrated. The Holocaust and the many subsequent genocidal wars, euphemistically called "ethnic cleansing," continue to emphasize man's murderous brutality to man!

What does this say to the serious-minded pastor? Hurting people in every congregation struggle with sin. Christian pastors, teachers and psychologists are awakening too late in many cases. Children are killing one another because of the meaninglessness brought to them by the pursuit of sin. Not every Christian is constantly struggling with terrible secret thoughts and sins, but I know that every Christian is tempted to sin and disobey God's revealed will in one way or another.

Even in the church, God's people fight a shame-filled battle against secret, and not-so-secret, sins. Many sit in God's house secretly condemned, and too often no one hears their cry for help! These born-again children of God know it is not right to be enslaved by the sins of the flesh. But they don't know how to handle them because no one has felt their pain or tried to help them! As pastors, we *must* tell them that after accepting Christ, they still have to deal with the temptations sin brings.

If we say that we have fellowship with Him, and walk in darkness, we lie and do not practice the truth. But if we walk in the light as He is in the light, we have fellowship with one another, and the blood of Jesus Christ His Son cleanses us from all sin.

If we say that we have no sin, we deceive ourselves, and the truth is not in us. If we confess our sins, He is faithful and just to forgive us our sins and to cleanse us from all unrighteousness. If we say that we have not sinned, we make Him a liar, and His word is not in us.

My little children, these things I write to you, so that you may not sin. And if anyone sins, we have an Advocate with the Father, Jesus Christ the righteous. And He Himself is the propitiation for our sins, and not for ours only but also for the whole world (1 John 1:6—2:2).

John's closing words, written around A.D. 90, show that he was speaking to Christians. We must *believe* and *know* that Christ is the propitiation for our sins, *but the temptation to sin has not been taken away. We will always have to deal with it!*

Regeneration makes new creatures of *every person* who comes to Christ. "Therefore, if anyone is in Christ, he is a new creation; old things have passed away; behold, all things have become new" (2 Corinthians 5:17).

After we are redeemed and placed in Christ, we have the power, freedom and ability to walk in the Spirit. We can fail to follow His inner leading, but once in Christ, we are no longer under condemnation for our old sins.

> There is therefore now no condemnation to them which are in Christ Jesus. . . . For the law of the Spirit of life in Christ Jesus hath made me free from the law of sin and death. For what the law could not do, in that it was weak through the flesh, God sending his own Son in the likeness of sinful flesh, and for sin, condemned sin in the flesh: that the righteousness of the law might be fulfilled in us, who walk not after the flesh, but after the Spirit. For they that are after the flesh do mind the things of the flesh; but they that are after the Spirit the things of the Spirit. For to be carnally minded is death; but to be spiritually minded is life and peace. Because the carnal mind is enmity against God: for it is not subject to the law of God, neither indeed can be. So then they that are in the flesh cannot please God (Romans 8:1-8, KJV).

Paul directed these remarks to those *in Christ Jesus*, and his instructions are clear. The believer *can* walk in the Spirit and not succumb to the temptations of his old nature, or "flesh." Holy living results from learning to walk in the Spirit.

When I was young, I earnestly sought a sanctifying visitation from God. One evening I received a touch that profoundly affected my senses. I was encouraged to claim it as an experience in holiness. As I continued my search for a spiritually triumphant lifestyle, however, my spirit became convicted that I was claiming a level of spirituality I had not reached. I still felt temptations which I was told I would never feel again.

The spiritual awakening did not give the insulation from temptation I had been taught to claim. Then I discovered that I had been looking back on an experience, rather than looking daily to the Holy Spirit for power to live victoriously over sin and temptation. With the deep shock of liberating truth, I realized that my professed level of personal holiness had been "experience-based."

During those days of youthful searching, a veteran teacher and preacher of the gospel spoke at a service I attended. His topic, "What Is Spirit-Led Living?" opened my eyes to my great error. I stopped looking back at my profound encounter and began looking unto Jesus, the author and finisher of my faith! (see Hebrews 12:2).

The freedom from condemnation that I began to experience is defined in Romans 8:1-5. It was an *exchanged life* experience in the Spirit for me. My struggle with temptation and sin did not stop, but my growth in true holiness in Christ began to move from inner victory to inner victory. I learned how important it is to recognize that I am "in Christ," rather than to depend on a wonderful experience that lasted less than an hour.

Years ago I met a man who publicly announced that he was so sanctified his "old man" was dead. I was confused. One of my mentors who had been in Christian ministry for nearly 60 years remarked, "Oh, don't let that bother you. Just hang around for a day or two and you will see that 'old man' resurrected!" What he said was true. I heard angry, uncontrolled words pour out of that man's mouth that were grossly untrue, uncalled-for, and certainly sinful!

How can we explain this situation to people? We are not saved by faith and grace alone, without works, then required to do all kinds of "good works" to maintain our salvation. We were regenerated "not by works of righteousness which we have done, but according to His mercy He saved us, through the washing of regeneration and renewing of the Holy Spirit" (Titus 3:5).

We are saved by grace, not works. We cannot presume to claim such self-developed faith that God recognized it and forgave us. "For by grace you have been saved through faith, and that not of yourselves; it is the gift of God, not of works, lest anyone should boast" (Ephesians 2:8, 9). Our justification is not maintained by post-regeneration works. "But to him who does not work but believes on Him who justifies the ungodly, his faith is counted for righteousness" (Romans 4:5).

God's grace doesn't teach a hopeless "sin-every-day religion." "For the grace of God that brings salvation has appeared to all men, teaching us that, denying ungodliness and worldly lusts, we should live soberly, righteously, and godly in the present age" (Titus 2:11, 12). What does the New Testament call believers? It calls them "saints." Not once in the New Testament are they called "sinners!" They are identified as being "carnal," "babes in Christ," "fleshly weak," and so forth, but never "sinners."

What about Paul's remarks in 1 Timothy 1:15: "This is a faithful saying and worthy of all acceptance, that Christ Jesus came into the world to save sinners, *of whom I am chief?*" This passage does not imply that Paul considered himself unchanged. He was not saying he still practiced sin. That would have denied his basic teachings on how a Christian should deal with sin.

> Likewise you also, reckon yourselves to be dead indeed to sin, but alive to God in Christ Jesus our Lord. Therefore do not let sin reign in your mortal body, that you should obey it in its lusts. And do not present your members as instruments of unrighteousness to sin, but present yourselves to God as being alive from the dead, and your members as instruments of righteousness to God. For sin shall not have dominion over you, for you are not under law but under grace (Romans 6:11-14).

Paul felt he had been one of the foremost sinners of his time. "You have heard of my former conduct in Judaism, how I persecuted the church of God beyond measure and tried to destroy it" (Galatians 1:13). When he referred to himself as "chief among sinners," he must have been powerfully moved by the memory of Christ's question to him on the Damascus road:

> As he journeyed he came near Damascus, and suddenly a light shone around him from heaven. Then he fell to the ground, and heard a voice saying to him, "Saul, Saul, why are you persecuting Me?"

And he said, "Who are You, Lord?"

Then the Lord said, "I am Jesus, whom you are persecuting. It is hard for you to kick against the goads" (Acts 9:3-5).

To have actually persecuted Israel's long-awaited Messiah was a haunting memory throughout Paul's Christian life. No wonder he felt as though he was chief among sinners. However, he told Roman and Corinthian believers that they had been "called to be saints" (Romans 1:7; 1 Corinthians 1:2). He addressed the "saints" in Achaia, Greece (2 Corinthians 1:1). Ephesians 1:1 addresses "the saints . . . in Ephesus." Philippians 1:1 says, "To all the saints in Christ Jesus who are in Philippi." Colossians 1:2 addresses "the saints and faithful brethren in Christ."

Paul's epistles show that while he called believers "saints," there were obvious imperfections, doctrinal errors, unacceptable practices, and even sin to be dealt with in their lives. Christian believers in the 21st century are like those of the first century—Christian saints under construction. From the moment of regeneration, the heavenly Father expects us to "grow in the grace and knowledge of our Lord and Savior Jesus Christ" (2 Peter 3:18).

The Bible says: "If we walk in the light, as He is in the light, we have fellowship one with another, and the blood of Jesus Christ His Son cleanses us from all sin" (1 John 1:7). The Greek tenses cause this promise to mean "*will be cleansing* us from all sin," in a continuing sense. We are, indeed, "saints under construction." Beginners and veterans, we grow at different rates.

No longer are we prisoners of the fallen nature *unless we submit to it.* As new creatures we can walk in the power of the Holy Spirit *if we wish to.* Temptation will always dog our steps; pastors know how true this is. But we can demand no more of the people than we do of ourselves. We must do all we can to help people walk in the light of Jesus Christ in their struggle against temptation.

Genuine, God-ordained pastoral ministry should be primarily focused on the *quality of spiritual life* among the people. Counseling programs that get down to basic issues are usually expressed by such questions as, "How do I really find out how to handle this kind of temptation?" Or, "How do I mend the fences I have broken down by my failure to walk in the Spirit?"

Since problems like these, and a thousand others, challenge us, are we really trying to walk with our people through their daily struggles? Are we bringing them under conviction and frustration while pretending to be spiritual conquerors, yet secretly battling our own difficulty? Leaving the impression that we are superhuman and easily walk through allurements unscathed and untempted is a pastoral error. We compound the problem when, without sensitivity and empathy, we chide our people for not living up to the standard we profess.

A young pastor's wife came to my office for counseling. She had come to the point that she was tired of always playing the hypocrite along with her husband. I asked her to clarify, and she said her husband went into the pulpit every week as though he were always intellectually and spiritually under control. "In truth," she said, "we are self-righteous frauds and I am so fed up with it that I hate going to church." She further revealed that the TV shows he watched at home bordered on pornography, and he was verbally abusive both to her and to their small son and daughter.

The pastor wouldn't come for counseling, and their home life was not one the parishioners would want to duplicate. I never saw him or his wife again, and I don't know what happened to them or their pastorate. I wonder how many other young pastors are practicing similar behavior in their churches. One thing I vividly remember: the wife said, "And in spite of all this sham, he tells people that he is a holiness preacher!"

In this book I examine the dangers of position, prestige and privilege. We must also be alerted to *pretension.* I lament a tragic drift away from honesty, holiness, and clean, moral behavior. With alarm I note that an emphasis on holiness is almost a thing of the past.

God's house has become an entertainment center where things said don't require holy living and thinking. The Lord's sanctuary functions as the theater, the social club and the gaming room. In many churches a decision for Christ is never encouraged or mentioned. We seem to have drifted far from Bible-centered thinking and living, forgetting the Scriptural injunction, "But as He who called you is holy, you also be holy in all your conduct, because it is written, 'Be holy, for I am holy!'" (1 Peter 1:15, 16).

The term *holiness* is seen as an archaic, monastic, outdated religious and social lifestyle embraced by modern hermits and social misfits. Instead, *holiness is still an expression of the character of God!* Regenerated Christians have accepted Christ, and His holiness was imputed to them! Like others, they struggle with temptation. The distinction is that they are new creatures in Christ through an act of God by the Holy Spirit.

Not all professing Christians avail themselves of the fullness of the Spirit's guidance. Those who do are not "improving" or "earning" their salvation. Yet, the Christian's reward at the judgment seat of Christ will be given accordingly. "For we must all appear before the judgment seat of Christ, that each one may receive the things done in the body, according to what he has done, whether good or bad" (2 Corinthians 5:10).

Eternal life doesn't depend on the outcome of this judgment. It will reveal *why* we performed certain works. It addresses reward for faithful ministry and service. Motives for seemingly righteous deeds will be revealed. After salvation by grace, our lives reveal how we use our "saved" status in serving God. His children must understand that the human quality of their work for Him will not be the criterion for God-given rewards. Man looks on the outward appearances, but God looks on the heart (1 Samuel 16:7).

I have known parishioners whose contribution to the life and ministry of the church was invaluable. When they didn't receive pastoral and public applause for it, they quit providing any service for God or His church. They had performed for human approbation alone. Self-worship, an insidious form of sin, violates the first commandment, "You shall have no other gods before Me" (Exodus 20:3).

An angel offered to take a self-important church worker to his mansion in heaven. As they passed exquisite mansions and the angel called out their owners, the man was excited. "Whose mansion is that?" he asked at an especially beautiful one. "Her earthly name was Sadie Jones," replied the angel. "She took in washing and cleaned houses for a living." The newly arrived church worker thought, *If Sadie Jones got that kind of a mansion, what must* mine *look like!* Soon they crossed the heavenly street and stopped before a humble cottage. "This is your mansion, sir," the angel said.

"There must be some mistake," the new arrival protested. "Everyone knew all the work I did for my church! My mansion should be 10 times the size of Sadie's!" The angel explained: "We build mansions with the materials Christians send up. Sadie Jones sent wonderful building materials with her self-sacrifice and humility. Your little cottage was built of *all* the materials you sent. You kept most of them on earth, receiving your praise and acclaim there, so we had nothing much to work with." People who work for their own glory are difficult to please or direct. Those who labor selflessly to build God's kingdom are a joy to every pastor.

When we permit people to work for the church, knowing the only reward they seek is the praise of people, we sin against them! As they get older and the years move them from the "laborers' limelight," they become bitter and resentful of both the church and fellow Christians.

> According to the grace of God which was given to me, as a wise master builder I have laid the foundation, and another builds on it. But let each one take heed how he builds on it. For no other foundation can anyone lay than that which is laid, which is Jesus Christ. Now if anyone builds on this foundation with gold, silver, precious stones, wood, hay, straw, each one's work will become clear; for the Day will declare it, because it will be revealed by fire; and the fire will test each one's work, of what sort it is. If anyone's work which he has built on it endures, he will receive a reward. If anyone's work is burned, he will suffer loss; but he himself will be saved, yet so as through fire (1 Corinthians 3:10-15).

God sees some who build on the foundation of Christ as builders using wood, hay and straw as construction materials. Their foundation is Christ, but their building materials are useless! At first I had difficulty discerning what Paul meant. Then I remembered useless works some of my ministering friends had performed, and things *I* did to please people rather than God. Sometimes my intentions were pure, but I lacked wisdom and my works produced disappointment. On other occasions my timing was wrong. Sometimes I had mixed motives: some things were done for God's glory and some for my own. These lapses have cost me rewards I shouldn't have lost.

I encourage every pastor to preach commendation and encouragement, rather than sin and condemnation. Since we have found Christ and He has found us, none of us has been perfect. Even the weakest, including those called into the ministry, are trying with the help of the Holy Spirit to walk in the light as He is in the light.

Emulate the Good Shepherd and lift up the sheep who are wounded. Don't help the devil do his soul-destroying work. Encourage people to be honest about their struggles. We do not always succeed, nor do our people.

> Who is he who condemns? It is Christ who died, and furthermore is also risen, who is even at the right hand of God, who also makes intercession for us (Romans 8:34).

Reach out to the defeated; pray with them. If you believe in holiness, put it into practice. Help people conquer sin in their daily lives.

CHAPTER 23

MOVING AGAINST DISTURBING TRENDS

Since its founding, the Christian church has been swimming against changing tides. This is true both in the secular and religious worlds. Dangerous trends have risen from within the community of the church itself. Astute godly leadership rose to the challenge to counteract such unscriptural inclinations.

Church history shows that when persecution of devout Christians existed, the church remained steadfast. Danger from non-Christian trends seems to appear when Christianity is generally accepted or at least peacefully tolerated.

A current problem is the serious lack of true Biblical knowledge among many younger Christians. They are usually sincere and idealistic, but they know much less than they should about the proper thought patterns and behavior of a Christian. A great percentage are victims of what I call "the majority mentality." It expresses itself in the concept that "since everyone is doing it, it must be acceptable in the sight of God."

During periods of religious acquiescence the church tends to grow numerically, but declines in purity of doctrine and quality of lifestyle. It becomes spiritually weak, doctrinally careless, morally disillusioned and increasingly tolerant of sin. The clear difference between professing Christians and the "decent" side of the secular world becomes so hazy that it is relatively indistinguishable.

Before we address the problems within the contemporary Christian church, however, we note the general "malaise" that plagues our nation today. This word is taken from two French words—*mal*, meaning "ill," and *aise*, meaning "feeling." Thus, *malaise* may be defined as "a vague feeling of unease, an unwholesome or undesirable state of affairs." It is generated, to a large degree, by a majority mentality, and seems to express itself in an effort to please everyone while claiming no moral or ethical standards.

At first glance, this philosophy may look clever. Wisdom demands that we take a serious second look, however, and analyze more deeply the behavior of "everyone" in the light of Luke 6:26: "Woe to you when all men speak well of you, for so did their fathers to the false prophets." Often, pastors and other leaders make the mistake of "going with the flow," rather than with those few who are struggling upstream. They do not consider the fact that all water, including sewage, finds the lowest possible level. Unfortunately, the lowest level is frequently the most popular. It requires minimal vision and offers no challenges morally, intellectually or spiritually.

This lifestyle results in a kind of self-indulgence that becomes the accepted way, rather than the best way—no questions asked. It is a comfortable state of affairs. People speak well of us when our philosophy doesn't trouble their consciences. We forget that the saying "Birds of a feather flock together" is true not only of pigeons or sparrows, but of vultures as well

As the years pass, we're forced to admit that the contemporary church is a multifaceted organism, congregating for various reasons and purposes. Sensationalism, religious entertainment, socialization, physical expressionism, borderline mysticism, and ethnic and sub-cultural religious forms are reasons for which we assemble.

Music in worship sessions covers the entire spectrum from soft rock to the ancient hymns of the Christian faith. Pulpit performances feature every form of elocution from grammatical stew to profound oratory—some is anointed and some is not. Churchgoers are offered a wide variety of worship diets. They can usually find some place where they feel at home and accepted if they search long enough. Why does a "majority mentality" exist, and why is it so widely accepted?

1. It is the easy way. It requires little in the way of moral or ethical self-discipline. Those who follow this way operate on the lowest level of reflection. They are often driven by lust and personal pleasure.

2. It meets little opposition from others. These individuals will not tolerate confrontation or questions about their pattern of behavior. Their thought train runs all the way from mental spine-less-ness and acquiescence to criminal rebellion and crime. They choose the path of least resistance and rest comfortably in it. We can be sure that we will not find their names or portraits enshrined in the great halls of liberty.

3. It is the road to popularity and political success. Understand that to be "politically correct" has nothing to do with being "morally correct." When the public shows no sense of outrage toward immorality in our leaders, is it because many of us are living or thinking by the same standards? We are at great risk of becoming a country governed by the mentality that "if everyone is

doing it, it can't be so wrong." We have become
calloused and insensitive to basic principles of
right and wrong. We must not forget that the
populace of a great nation was led into a state of
near mass hypnosis by the Nazi philosophy that
it was acceptable to exterminate people whose
fundamental beliefs were contrary to the "party
line" or "the good of the country." Hundreds of
thousands of human lives were sacrificed. Jesus
made the issue clear:

> "Enter by the narrow gate; for wide is the gate and
> broad is the way that leads to destruction, and there
> are many who go in by it. Because narrow is the gate
> and difficult is the way which leads to life, and there
> are few who find it" (Matthew 7:13, 14).

4. It is the path of flexibility. Many who hold
to the majority mentality may not wish to accept
Jesus' word for it. However, without the discipline to stick to a plain "yes" or "no" in our responses, our word is meaningless (5:37). There
is nothing to bind us in friendship, marriage or
business. Indeed, no news report or any other
method of sharing facts is credible alongside a
double-talk syndrome.

When ethics become situational, our reputa-
tions as people of integrity go quickly down the
social and commercial drain. Jesus was saying
that anything short of transparent honesty and
integrity originates from evil.

When a person's word becomes questionable,

it is worthless and so is his or her name. Even one's signature lacks value. One's true worth will sooner or later become apparent to others. Nothing said or done will ever be taken seriously again.

5. It eases an already fickle and flighty conscience. The evasion of simple truth is the shortest road to catastrophe for any relationship, whether marital, social or political. In the offender's mind, wrongdoing becomes right-doing and the action becomes honest, ethical and acceptable by any standard. We who are charged with the responsibility of leading must avoid and renounce this trend with every ounce of influence we possess.

Let us not be misled by what is called the "popular vote." Unless the vote is based on the sound principles of justice and truth for all, it is nothing less than a majority mentality based on injustice, immorality and deceit. Through human history, those who have adopted the majority mentality have found themselves in predicaments they never anticipated.

Serious Christian leadership often discerns this fateful degeneration, but history reveals that just as often people have taken the wrong course to correct the problems. In the church we have enhanced programs, changed worship forms, introduced new Bible study series and reorganized the already over-organized organization.

Sometimes leadership blames the laity for the decline, while the laity blames the leadership.

Only truth sets men free. The truth, therefore, is the only liberating agent for those who have fallen prey to this error.

The "wide gate" is not the road to true and lasting success. If there is fame, prosperity or status to be gained, it will be because we endeavored to take the road to moral and spiritual success by entering through the unpopular, but narrow, gate. Remember: *Right is right, even if everyone is against it; wrong is wrong, even if everyone is for it.*

Jesus said, "And I, if I am lifted up from the earth, will draw all peoples to Myself" (John 12:32). The basic issue, then, is not the form of worship, nor the music, nor the preaching style. The issue in the mind of God is "Did the worshipers meet *Me*?"

Is Christ exalted and His presence experienced by the worshipers in your church? Is the worship a genuinely spiritual and moving event, or merely an exciting social experience?

In whose presence do the people revel? Is it in God's presence? Or is it in the presence of our religious, socializing friends?

219

CHAPTER 24

DISSIDENCE: DESTROYER OF UNITY AND FELLOWSHIP

*A*s I meditated over the future of Christian ministries, I became convinced that if they ever disintegrate and cease to exist, it will be due to errors from within their own structures, rather than from satanic forces without. For some time I looked for a powerful word to express a warning to the body of Christ. Finally, I settled on the word *dissidence*. The dictionary defines *dissidence* as "conflict, discord or disharmony." For our purposes, I will define it as "that insidious habit of picking imaginary holes in another leader's methods or doctrinal position behind his back, so that the leader has no opportunity to explain his position or defend it." When we are more impressed with what we *think we know* than with what we *realize we don't know*, we reach a point of moral, spiritual and intellectual peril.

Here are some insidious causes that spawn the evil of dissidence.

Intellectual Arrogance

This sin has been a curse to Christian fellowship and unity from the very beginning. The apostle Paul declared, "And if anyone thinks that he knows anything, he knows nothing yet as he ought to know" (1 Corinthians 8:2).

I discovered this truth when I first entered college. I was humiliated by my common farm background and what seemed to me at the time to be the ignorance of my parents. After graduation I was utterly amazed at how much they had learned while I was away.

Dogmatic Legalism

Legalism is always demanding and pervasive. It caters to one's ego. I have met men and women in ministry who seemed to believe they were God's last word of revelation to the human family, and they were quick to express that belief. Many of them have written books on church building and church growth, but their own churches do not model that growth. Indeed, some have ceased to exist altogether and their founders are now pursuing mundane careers far from the realms of ministry. Christianity is not held together by unanimity of all doctrine, but by unanimity of the Spirit. If we ever forget this salient fact, we will be doomed to spiritual extinction.

We are essentially a social religion built around redemption in Christ Jesus. To try to turn Christianity into a solitary, doctrinaire movement will either destroy the faith or reduce it to a set of Christless and legalistic dos and don'ts.

The curse of dissidence has existed since the Christian church began. Archbishop Cranmer wrote in 1552 that nothing caused more separation in the church than disputes and critical remarks made by one leader about another—especially disputes concerning varied practices which were, in themselves, not unscriptural. He declared on the other hand that nothing maintained unity and defended the fold of Christ more than the pure teaching of the gospel and harmony in fellowship.

We are all aware of the minor differences that exist in our interpretations of Scripture and the practice of Christian church polity (not policy). But it is the *basic doctrine* of the Christian faith that unites us. The cardinal doctrines of redemption, justification, propitiation and regeneration are the great links that hold the people of God together. To avoid contentious and divisive remarks concerning our insignificant differences in worship

forms, minor doctrinal variations, Scriptural interpretations and practices is nothing less than a basic survival technique.

Unity is greater than *union*, and *communion* is
greater than *cooperation* and *perfunctory together-
ness*. The church must continually embrace the
common principles of old-fashioned Christianity revealed in the New Testament. These alone should
distinguish us from other forms of religion. We who
claim His name must remember that He prayed
for us to be *one* (see John 17:11, 21, 22).

Further, God's Word declares us to be one in
Christ. To be in Christ is to be one with everyone
who is in Him. Even within denominations we find
more competition than cooperation. This tends to distance one from another and both from the leading
of the Holy Spirit. Of course there will be distinc-
tions and varied emphases of truth, but they are
for the purpose of establishing identity.

Change is an element of growth, and not some
new ground for judgmentalism. We must keep discord out of the process as we grow in our knowledge of God, His Word and His character. Change
came in Paul's life and philosophy during his days
in the desert of Arabia (see Galatians 1:17, 18). Those
who accepted the transformed Saul of Tarsus were
blessed by his revelation of a new plan of God that
was different from Judaism.

If we recognize that changes are inevitable, we

must be prepared to accept them in the spirit of wisdom. Avoid disharmony at all cost. Future significant changes which the Holy Spirit may lead us to make should be done with prayer and maintained in faith. Privately, we must remember that *all* Christian leaders go through times of isolation as we move in the ever-growing realm of eternal values and spiritual truths.

During those lonely moments, we must not fall to the temptation of believing that somehow this makes us spiritually superior to others. Satan will take advantage of solitary moments of spiritual ecstasy to introduce us to the notion that we have reached some peak of unusual spiritual excellence. This, in turn, leads us to criticize those he suggests are not as spiritual as we are. Church leadership must adopt a new motto:

In essentials, unity;
In non-essentials, liberty;
In diversity, charity;
In all things, Christ first.

Regardless of how diligent you may be in discharging your pastoral duties, you will serve some ungrateful people who may maltreat you and speak disparagingly of you. Yet, you are under divine orders to support them and pray for them. Some of your people may express unscriptural ideas and objectives that you know are wrong. Do not, either privately or publicly, utter critical remarks about them.

Pray for them. They are not your enemies; they are your sheep.

When we make disparaging remarks about another Christian—whether leader or layman—time alone may embarrass us. When I was younger I criticized the actions and decisions of some of my brethren. As the "University of Time" carried me from one experience to another, I realized that my unkind remarks were made from my own lack of knowledge and experience. I had to ask for God's forgiveness and apologize to those whom I had tried to belittle.

If you have had more experience in certain fields of Christian endeavor than other people, give them time to learn before you criticize them. I have known younger men who, while struggling to please God and win the souls of men, became demoralized by those who should have been helping them.

A young couple drove 600 miles to pour out their discouragement to me. They had graduated from a good ministerial training institute and the husband was serving as a junior assistant to an older pastor. He did an outstanding job with the youth department until the senior pastor became jealous of his success and began uttering disparaging remarks about him. The young assistant endured until the pastor's jealousy caused him to trump up a trivial charge against the man and dismiss him from his church. Brokenhearted, this couple wept in my office, not understanding why they had suffered this kind of treatment.

I questioned them lovingly, but intensely, to test the depth of their divine call. They came through with a tearfully powerful response. Then I suggested they return to where the wife's parents lived, locate a new subdivision with little Christian activity, and begin a Bible study group with a few friends of their own age. I assured them it would most likely develop into a small congregation.

I did not hear from them for nearly four years. One day I received a telephone call telling me they were dedicating their new church with nearly 250 members! Had I not poured the oil of encouragement on that young disillusioned couple, the heartless, un-Christian actions of a senior pastor would have driven them from Christian ministry.

It is tragic that the same tongue that utters sermons of love and goodness also can utter epithets of criticism and disparagement against another servant of God.

The psalmist had that problem with people who sometimes pretended to be his friends. David wrote, "Your tongue devises destruction, like a sharp razor, working deceitfully" (Psalm 52:2). Dissidence is a cruel and character-marring kind of untruth that can be rectified only by the person uttering it. May God help us to remember that words can heal and words can wound.

God hears the sweet-sounding words men speak. He notes as well the barbed innuendos that are so thinly veiled behind hypocritical smiles. Our words, after all, are expressions that are generated in our hearts and minds. They reflect our real character and the depth of our professed sincerity.

When spoken in bitterness or resentment, they are like the dagger of an assassin, murdering another Christian servant's reputation and character. Jesus said:

> "But I say to you that for every idle word men may speak, they will give account of it in the day of judgment. For by your words you will be justified, and by your words you will be condemned" (Matthew 12:36, 37).

Cruel and destructive remarks about another arise from jealousy, spiritual weakness, cowardice and concealed hatred. If we cannot say uplifting and encouraging words about God's people and our fellow workers, let us be silent until the Holy Spirit takes control of our thoughts.

The words that spew out of our mouths can, and do, wreak havoc, conflict, discord and disharmony in the body of Christ. "Brethren, these things ought not to be so" (James 3:10).

CHAPTER 25

A Hard Look at Congregational Autonomy

When we study the first Christian congregations, we have to acknowledge two basic facts. The first is that of their autonomy. They struggled and survived in situations that were peculiar to their own unique geographic and ethnic community. Second, they recognized a spiritual unity. This existed because of the influence of the evangelistic and apostolic leadership through which they were developed.

What we have long called "denominationalism" was unknown to them. They assisted one another financially just as the Gentile churches sent aid to the poor saints in Jerusalem. Each congregation became aware of the fact that it was not alone in the Roman world. It saw its evangelistic responsibilities in the context of "Jerusalem, Judea, Samaria, and the ends of the earth."

The early churches knew that Christ died in Jerusalem for the whole world, yet that city soon ceased to be recognized as the heart of the first-century church. Other cities like Antioch and Ephesus developed Christian congregations while the Jewish-Roman conflict left Jerusalem in rubble, its people dispersed, and caused the city's influence on the church to wane. Scripturally, either congregational independence or an early form of denominationalism truly existed.

As a senior servant of Christ, I understand why sincere pastors and their people sometimes leave historic denominations. Often there are good reasons, but there are also dangers. Every Christian congregation, whether or not denominationally aligned, develops only by the quality of its Christianity in its respective community. If it does not make an impact in its own "Jerusalem," it will never reach its Samaria *or* the ends of the earth.

Reasons for congregational failure are many. Some congregations and their pastors go independent in the hope that it will solve what they see as problems. Others find it necessary to make their departure because of rigid and graceless denominational pressures.

In the last congregation I served as associate

pastor, a few of our parishioners suggested that we should consider leaving our denomination. However, we loved our church and its worldwide outreach, as well as the opportunity it offered to minister as we felt led of the Lord. We refused to consider such a move and chose instead to remain in fellowship and try to effect change for the better in our denomination.

Our choice proved to be wise. We saw the Holy Spirit bring about many changes in outdated concepts and methods. Denominational leadership came to see that change does not always mean unscriptural compromise or a step toward apostasy.

Not all decisions for congregational independence are based on godly wisdom and Biblical truth, yet they still persist. It is therefore necessary for every pastor or congregation contemplating this move to spend much time in prayer and in counsel with God's veterans before doing so. I list some of the more prevalent reasons pastors and congregations consider independence.

Pastoral Inadequacy

My heart goes out to those who take on a charge they are incapable of handling. In most cases the person feels he can do the job, but such deficiencies as weakness in public speaking or lack of training and essential giftings cause the pastoral task to overwhelm him. Perhaps he inspires the people to believe in his calling, as well as in abilities he does not possess. When the congregation realizes he has oversold himself, he often blames the failure on denominational affiliation. All of us in Christ's service must bear in mind that a person is not a failure until he blames another for his mistakes. It is much worse when in our hearts we secretly blame *God* for our mistakes.

A Christian layman complained bitterly to me about the performance of his pastor. I am not sure all of his complaints arose from actual facts, but they serve to illustrate my point. It sounded like the classic case of a pastor taking on more than he could handle. The man was raised on a mission field where his parents labored in the Third World. Consequently, he grew up among uneducated people living slightly above the poverty level. They were incapable of taking a leadership role among their fellow Christian converts.

Now, in a civilized and highly developed country, he seldom bothered to visit the sick and aging among his people. He couldn't tolerate anyone on his staff with leadership qualities that he did not possess, and subsequently fired several of his most capable staff members. He preached quite well, I was told, but his messages were not Bible-based. He preferred to base them on movies he had been watching! He had depleted the local church's treasury by more than a million dollars and their funds were almost gone. He had lost most of the gifted men on his staff and church council. The music department had lost many of its best musicians and singers.

When I heard this heartbreaking story, I thought of the many dedicated people who were affected. Similar situations occur elsewhere, and they are all classic cases of "pastoral inadequacy" or leadership confusion and immaturity.

Problems of Denominational Alignment

I have observed congregations which, due to scholarly Biblical leadership, have moved away from some legalistic and archaic concepts to a more Scriptural and orthodox interpretation of the gospel. When these liberating truths bring a congregation to a renewed spiritual life and vitality, nothing should hinder them.

If denominational leadership holds dogmatically to certain antiquated and unscriptural concepts, and attempts to force it on a Biblically awakened congregation, only two alternatives remain. Either the denomination softens its demands and accepts new Scriptural light, or the congregation must disassociate itself. This disassociation is not based on pastoral popularity, finances, church politics or anything but truth—Biblical truth alone.

The Deadly Superiority Complex

Over my years of service I have seen this ugly form of self-aggrandizement show itself in many pastoral situations. Some of my own students, despite my most earnest efforts to help them, have caught this prideful malady. It is a sinister form of self-worship that renders a man or woman unwilling to take advice from anyone. It is a form of arrogance that often looks upon itself as God's last word of wisdom and counsel to the human race.

Some pastors infected by this superiority complex have abandoned their association with a denomination because of it. God's Word declares, "Pride goes before destruction, and a haughty spirit before a fall" (Proverbs 16:18). A good command of the language, a sparkling personality or an overpowering persuasiveness are not substitutes for sincerity and genuineness.

The man who presents himself as God's servant must prove he is a servant. If a pastor will accept counsel and conduct a self-initiated program of true self-assessment, he will discover many humbling surprises. If we, as professed men of God, try to play games with God, our self-centered facade will be discerned by our parishioners.

A student with an unusually high level of self-confidence concerned me. He accepted a small pastorate, and I asked a church member how he was doing. The parishioner hesitated in giving a direct answer, but when he realized how forthright I had been in my question, he said, "Well, Dr. McLuhan, if I could buy him for what he is worth and sell him for what he thinks he is worth,

I would be a rich man!" That was all the answer I needed. This terrible spiritual illness causes a leader to cut all fellowship ties, rather than submit to the kind counsel of superiors. It brings that person pastoral rejection and fruitless isolation. If we cannot *take* advice, we will never have the maturity to *give* it.

If we choose the lonely, arrogant road of imagined social and spiritual superiority, we will end our journey alone. Self-worship brings self-destruction from the hands of its own god.

Insatiable Greed

Paul wrote something all pastors should heed:

> For the love of money is the root of all evil; which while some coveted after, they have erred from the faith, and pierced themselves through with many sorrows (1 Timothy 6:10, KJV).

Money in itself is not evil, but the *love* of money is mammon worship. Paul said in verse 5 that the proof of a corrupt mind in false religious leaders is the idea that financial gain is a sign or proof of godliness. The love of money is a violation of the first of the Ten Commandments: "You shall have no other gods before Me!" (Exodus 20:3).

Some pastors break away from denominational ties because independence gives them a position in which they are no longer accountable to others in reporting their actual income from God's people. Some have made themselves rich in the world's goods at the cost of the true spiritual leadership of their people. Money at its best is nothing less than "filthy lucre" (KJV). Both Paul and Peter addressed this problem (see 1 Timothy 3:3, 8; Titus 1:7; 1 Peter 5:2).

Contemporary church management proves that both denominational affiliation and congregational autonomy work well. Truly great and successful congregations are growing and doing the work of Christ in both camps. Studies show that neither independence nor denominational association causes congregational success. Nor has a particular mode of operation proven to be truly God's way with His people. The real issue is how effective the church is in the following principles.

1. The pastor and staff must develop a plan of ministry that parishioners understand and support. In my last assignment I discovered anew how important a long-range plan is. Our goal was not merely to make the congregation happy and satisfied, but to develop them into a genuine ministering community, a people useful in God's kingdom. It took several years to move the congregation from merely coming to church to get a blessing. They learned, however, that *being* a blessing was much more satisfying than *getting* a blessing.

This church became a real, caring community which led the people to extend compassionate Christian ministry to those who needed it. This was in a great church with between 12,000 and 15,000 members. The senior pastor continually emphasized the ministry of God's people to others. This concept was embraced by hundreds who found that they too had a ministry.

In the midst of a service, people would be asked to raise their hands if they had a need or were hurting. Others were encouraged to move close to those people and minister spiritually. I clearly remember a man who had been a faithful Christian for years coming to me in tears after a service. He said, "This is the first time that I have attended a church where I felt I had a ministry and was needed." He and his wife were still worshiping there when I retired.

A church without a goal or objective in ministry will go nowhere. Its people will become as dissatisfied as one trying to walk endlessly on a treadmill of merely religious activity. This is true of both an independent congregation and of one denominationally aligned.

2. The pastor and staff must observe the difference between religious celebration and genuine worship. There is a significant difference between the fellowship hall and the sanctuary. Joining friends for a happy songfest is not the same as coming into the awe-inspiring presence of God to worship in humility and penitence. Humans are social beings, but a relationship with God must be more than a mere social experience. Every pastor and staff should emphasize the sacredness and holiness of God's house. When worshipers come to church only to meet friends and hear an emotionally titillating sermon, they have not truly come to meet God.

I must emphasize that a well-chosen organ or piano prelude in the sanctuary greatly assists in creating an atmosphere of worship in the sanctuary, even when more contemporary music follows. Sadly, many professing Christians have never discovered exactly who God is and how to worship Him. Being independent or denominationally affiliated has nothing to do with making His house a holy sanctuary in our spiritual experience.

3. The pastor and staff must faithfully and without compromise preach the Word. The Holy Scriptures must always be the major emphasis in both the worship services and training schedules. Sincere worshipers do not come to God's house to hear a political lecture or a treatise on human behavior. These tell what *man* thinks. The Bible brings us face-to-face with who God is and how He thinks about us, His children. He is concerned with our lives in their changing vicissitudes, and provides us with words of comfort and guidance in every human situation.

In recent years I have been struck with the fact that many Christian songwriters seem to know little about the truths of God's Word. Their lyrics reflect Biblical ignorance. Unfortunately, both independent and denominationally aligned congregations sing songs devoid of Scriptural content. Many choruses sung in the contemporary church are so unscripturally based that they border on heresy. Yet they are sung with gusto by people to whom the Bible is an unknown entity. Its comforting and encouraging message is never defined.

4. The pastor and staff must feel the social and spiritual pulse of the contemporary world. A wise man said, "Preach to hurting people and you'll always have an audience." I have listened to contemporary preachers who seemed to be living in another world. They addressed none of the hurts or pains of men and women in today's society. Sadly, thousands of lonely, hurting listeners turn off their radios or television sets because the speaker has not established a communicative bridge upon which he or she could lead them to hope, forgiveness and peace.

God's leaders who have never learned to weep with those who weep will never have the reward of rejoicing with those who rejoice. I have learned that, as a Christian, my ministry must be to both living and dying humanity. Every pastor's goal is a congregation that develops saints who are growing. People who are not fed from God's Word never grow.

The congregation that sets up a solid, progressive and acceptable Bible study program will sooner or later draw and hold people. This is true in

Parents who have know Christ long enough to think about their children's faith will insist on a sound Biblical Christian education program.

Every alert pastor realizes that, for the most part, he is attempting to lead and teach a congregation among which there are many Biblical illiterates. I was amazed at a pastor friend who lamented this fact. He remarked, "My people are wonderful, but many of them are so Biblically ignorant that they think the Epistles are the sons and daughters of the apostles!"

Skilled teaching from the cradle roll to the adult Bible classes is essential. It is more lasting and effective than an expensive, scintillating entertainment-type service which is quickly forgotten. We must strive to have a lasting impact on those who come to worship and learn about the faith. Nothing accomplishes this as well as systematic Bible teaching, skillfully presented to every age group.

A wisely planned local church program may include entertainment, but its primary focus must be inspiration, information, fellowship, counseling and the involvement of its people. Paul defines the purpose of apostolic and pastoral leadership in the congregation: "For the perfecting of the saints, for the work of the ministry, for the edifying of the body of Christ" (see Ephesians 4:11, 12, KJV). One would have to perform some extraordinary interpretive gymnastics to find entertainment a primary responsibility of leadership in Christ's church!

The Word of God presented with power and skill is entertainment enough. Preaching the truths of God's Word is the prime task of every man and woman called to pastoral ministry or evangelism. Let us educate our people and their families in the truths of God's Word.

Understand my heart's passion on the issue of congregational independence versus denominational affiliation. Over the years I have had opportunity to minister in both camps and to share in-depth with pastors. I understand why some have departed from their denominations and why others are still happily and successfully involved in theirs. I have come to the conclusion that God does not really care in which camp a pastor and his people are serving Him. I have no regrets or personal spiritual discomfort when one of my former students abandon congregational affiliation.

One of my most-gifted young graduates in South Africa left his denomination and he and his people have developed a thriving, spiritually alive church. It has become a respected blessing in the community. Others have stuck fast to their original denominational commitment and developed congregations equally successful. My heart has truly ached for those wonderful young men who made one move or the other with their congregations, but did not succeed. Somewhere they made a mistake. Why did these people fail?

The answer to this question is found in my reason for writing this book. I recall tearfully a young man who was doing quite well in a denominational setting. He had experienced a few difficulties, but nothing unusual or limited to his own unhappy experiences. In spite of counsel from many of his friends and superiors, he took his congregation out of its parent denomination. The result was tragic. Independence resulted in a number of difficult situations he did not foresee. He became frustrated. His people became confused and discouraged. What had looked like a church with real promise literally fell apart at the seams. I weep for him and his godly wife.

Similarly, I have been associated with a promising young man who, though raised in a denominational setting, departed from it. He had a tremendous vision for his new congregation, but complete independence took him by surprise. He envisioned starting many sister churches in his area, but the opposite has taken place. Without the guidance of experienced Christian veterans to help him, it will only be a matter of time until he will be relieved of his charge and dismissed. I am saddened by the entire scenario; he was one of my students. What will he and his wife and family do? What will be the long-term effect of this failure upon the congregation?

On the other hand, I have seen a pastor who, with his congregation, left a well-organized and successful form of congregational independence to join a denomination. The move was heralded with a great prayer meeting and a lot of rejoicing over their expected enlarged fellowship opportunities. Unfortunately, they had been so used to making decisions for themselves that the guidance offered by the denomination was mistaken for interference.

I know the situation very well, and know that the advice that seemingly threatened them was given in good faith and for their own benefit. The congregation split over the issue. Now there are two confused and impotent congregations worshiping in two struggling churches. Someone missed the leading of the Spirit and the mind of God.

To sum it up, a Christian pastor is a person who must know, love and communicate in three dimensions: with God, with people and with himself. He must be true to each of these. If he fails to recognize who each really is, he will fail. God alone has no limitations; He alone does not sin.

The pastor's responsibility is to bring himself and his people into the presence of God. He must possess the gentleness of Christ. He soon learns that God's sheep are different from normal, earthly sheep. Some of them *bite* and do other unkind things.

Like their shepherd, however, they are moving from a life of sin and unbelief onward and upward toward the image of Christ. Permit the Holy Spirit to help you model godliness at a level they can follow.

God will enable you to do it!

CHAPTER 26

FANATICISM, SECULARISM AND FAITH INTERPRET TRAGEDY

*P*eriodic earthquakes, floods, and the El Niño and La Niña phenomena have plagued humanity from ancient history until this hour. All of these occurrences raise the serious question, "How does a Christian interpret and face natural tragedies?"

Years ago, Bob Ingersol, a noted atheist, implied at the funeral of his brother that in spite of all the joy and love expressed in the human experience, the great tragedy of death ended the story of life with stark mystery. His only view of human existence was secular, physical and sentient, a view still held by many in the world.

This concept deliberately leaves the impression that there is no God, no eternal life and no future. It suggests that death is a final, blind leap into the unknown abyss of undefined nihilism. Yet, many illusionary dreamers believe that God does exist and is working behind the changing fortunes of humanity in an unknown and mystical way. In fact, a recent poll discovered that 90 percent of Americans believe in God.

Like pagans of old, they interpret earthquakes, volcanoes, floods and other catastrophes as signs of God's implacable anger at humanity for both societal and personal sins. Theirs is a physical religion of terror that leaves man responsible for tragedy but powerless to do anything about it.

In a few places in the world, primitive people still offer sacrifices in an attempt to appease the wrath of an unknown deity. But God is not a capricious judge who takes pleasure in punishing His children; everything He does has purpose.

Then there is the fanatic. His God is a pitiless and graceless deity of revenge and judgment. He looks at disasters as undeniable proof of God's anger at human failure. He smugly views them as opportunities to prove his own particular philosophy. He emphasizes that this is what he himself had foretold would happen.

Years ago I counseled a young woman who, after several unfruitful counseling sessions, seemed to be getting nowhere. I asked her to write her concept of God, and she wrote: "God is a great all-knowing judge who watches and notes my every move so that one day in the courts of His divine justice He can bring up every charge against me and condemn me to a burning hell." Though religious, she was a fanatic who misinterpreted who God is and what He's like.

Anyone familiar with the Scriptures knows that unexplained pain and sorrow come to many of God's followers. Job experienced inexplicable domestic tragedy to a degree that few of us have had to face. His comforters, like today's counterparts, were sure God had permitted, or even caused, Job's calamities because of secret sins in his life. The reason was veiled in the inscrutable plan of a sovereign God. Job wasn't perfect, but his problems were not the result of his imperfections. Neither are yours and mine. Terrible things happen which can't be blamed on human faults or secret sins.

Some friends suffered terribly when a loved one was in a two-car collision. A family member asked if I thought God let the crash happen because of sin in the lives of those involved. I assured her that neither God nor an angel drove those cars. In all probability it was simple human error or carelessness that caused the collision.

Jesus emphasized this truth in Luke 13:2-5. He spoke of Galilean worshipers who, in the midst of their sacrifices, were attacked by Roman soldiers.

Pontius Pilate mixed their blood with the blood of the sacrifice. Jesus also spoke of a tragedy that took place in or near the tower of Siloam in Jerusalem. It collapsed and killed 18 people. Jesus pointed out that neither the murdered worshipers nor the people on whom the tower fell were necessarily wicked. In a physical world we experience physical tragedies that have nothing whatsoever to do with our spiritual condition.

Starry-eyed, professing Christian prophets teach that the Christian life must always be an experience of unruffled happiness. They never understand that unexpected tragedy for saints takes place simply because we live in an environment that is fraught with danger. Often nothing could have been done to prevent the calamity. The level of godliness in the victims had nothing to do with the event.

Our bodies are temples of the Holy Spirit, but they are made of perishable material. We have to keep them from danger. They grow older with time—Paul reminds us that our outer man perishes day by day (2 Corinthians 4:16). An 80-year-old may pray for good health, but he cannot expect to receive 25-year-old good health. Being godly does not remove us from the realities and risks of the physical world. If genuine faith immunized believers from accidents, epidemics, aging and physical tragedy, the world would have embraced Christianity long ago. The Word says:

> "As I live," says the Lord God, "I have no pleasure in the death of the wicked, but that the wicked turn from his way and live" (Ezekiel 33:11).
>
> The Lord is not slack concerning His promise, as some count slackness, but is longsuffering toward us, not willing that any should perish but that all should come to repentance (2 Peter 3:9).

God is not striding across the earth using natural disasters, accidents or disease to punish sinners and faltering saints. Christ paid our debts for us on the cross. God promises to protect and care for us. It is important to remember, however, that if we ignore or flaunt His laws, our physical bodies will ultimately suffer the consequences. These hard facts still stand unshaken and unchanged before us:

- The *Jameses* still die by Herod's sword, but the *Peters* are delivered from prison and certain death.

- Faithful *Jonathans* still die by the sword of the Philistines, while the *Isaiahs* are still being sawed in two by pagan God-haters.

- The *Peters* may still endure crucifixion, heads down, and the *Pauls* close out their magnificent lives of evangelism at Nero's execution block.

- More timely, lovely churches of faithful Guatemalans are torn to shreds by a devastating hurricane, while churches that are apostate stand untouched and unscathed.

- Many of God's people are starving to death in a world of plenty because they live in a land where there are pockets of poverty.

- In recent years the Christian church has suffered more martyrs than it has for 10 centuries. At the same time it is seeing unprecedented revival and growth.

To the Christian, tragedy is an ever-present possibility. God can, and sometimes does, prevent it; but He does not always do so. Christians must face the possibility of tragedy with faith and responsibility. We have the blessed assurance of God's promise that, for those who love Him and are called according to His purpose, He will make all things—even tragedies—work out for good (see Romans 8:28).

In the face of heartache, pain and loss, we have Someone to turn to. We can reach up and grasp the unseen hand and walk with God through the tempest of anguish and grief—even the valley of the shadow of death itself. This makes true Christian faith unique in the realm of unexplained and unexpected human disaster.

CHAPTER 27

WHY WE NEED A CODE OF ETHICS

*M*any people, including some Christian pastors, reject the idea of being governed by any form of discipline that has been set up by anyone but themselves. They follow no form of ordered lifestyle. They boast of freedom to act and speak as they feel. But we must declare that they are subject to the laws of God as defined in His Word. They need to follow a code of ethics.

What do we mean by a "code of ethics"? The Greek word *ethikos*, from which our English word *ethics* originates, has to do with the demonstration of character. The word *ethics* is used in a number of ways. A dictionary defines it as "the rules of conduct recognized in respect to a particular class of human actions." We speak of "medical ethics" for physicians and practitioners and "business ethics" for men and women in the business world. Violators of ethical standards may not always suffer punishment by the law, but they lose the respect and trust of those to whom ethical behavior is important. Someone once said, "True freedom is in learning to live comfortably in one's harness."

Not all ethical criteria are in print, but there is a need for certain standards to be put into recorded form. Human memory demands a constant reminder, and if a group of people wishes to set up a fellowship, a company, an organization or a community, basic rules must be documented. God proved this when He gave us the Ten Commandments. Humanity had to have fundamental guidance in what He, their Creator, expected of them.

It is important to understand that we are not saved by obeying a moral or spiritual code. We are enabled to adhere to that moral or spiritual code *because* we are saved. Our salvation is demonstrated by our behavior. Jesus said, "Let your light so shine before men, that they may see your good works and glorify your Father in heaven" (Matthew 5:16). Good works are not performed for God's benefit. He knows exactly who and what we are. Obedience to a higher code of moral, spiritual and ethical behavior is our most powerful testimony.

What makes us different? We are different because we have a freedom that enables us to live triumphantly without obvious struggle and rigorous self-discipline. The Holy Spirit enables us to live this way because God is glorified by Spirit-empowered standards of behavior. We are painfully aware that living up to God's divine expectations is a constant challenge. It is accomplished only in the power of the Holy Spirit.

Our problem is that often we find ourselves trying to occupy the driver's seat. The pressure exerted on us by the world, the flesh and the devil urges us to "take control!" But the power of God's code is His voice saying, "This is what your life could be if you would let Me live it through you."

To intellectually accept a lofty code of ethics does not mean that we ourselves measure up to God's standards in spirit, mind and action. In fact, accepting the code may become a form of self-justification as we deceive ourselves into believing that knowledge of ethical and spiritual standards is proof that we actually live by them. *Motives* are the key to eternal rewards:

> For we are God's fellow workers; you are God's field, God's building. By the grace God has given me, I laid a foundation as an expert builder, and someone else is building on it. But each one should be careful how he builds. For no one can lay any foundation other than the one already laid, which is Jesus Christ. If any man builds on this foundation using gold, silver, costly stones, wood, hay or straw, his work will be shown for what it is, because the Day will bring it to

> light. It will be revealed with fire, and the fire will test
> the quality of each man's work. If what he has built
> survives, he will receive his reward. If it is burned up,
> he will suffer loss; he himself will be saved, but only
> as one escaping through the flames (1 Corinthians
> 3:9-15, *NIV*).

Paul did not imply that eternal life was the
reward for using the right materials. Salvation
is a gift, not a reward. God will not ask *what* we
have done, He will ask *why* we did it. Although
saved by grace, we may be building our own pride
of doctrine, our quality of work or our excellence
of performance and giving. It may be for hardship
endured on the mission field.

> With this in mind, we constantly pray for you, that
> our God may count you worthy of his calling, and
> that by his power he may fulfill every good pur-
> pose of yours and every act prompted by your faith.
> We pray this so that the name of our Lord Jesus
> may be glorified in you, and you in him, according
> to the grace of our God and the Lord Jesus Christ
> (2 Thessalonians 1:11, 12, *NIV*).

Our code of Christian ethics, then, determines
our motives. Success in following it is clearly
revealed in the answer to this question: *Who is
being praised and glorified by all my labors? Is it I,
or the Lord God Almighty?*

CHAPTER 28

CHURCH STAFF ETHICS

*T*o be a shepherd of souls, the most-needed strength is the knowledge of God. The next need is a deep desire to know and love those with whom you work to shepherd God's sheep. I have always felt that every Bible college, seminary and theological school should feature a training program for future ministers teaching them how to work with others on a team.

Those called of God into Christian service always have varied gifts and talents, but they are called to work together. Too many times Christian workers compete more than they cooperate. Both harmony and peace are essential to success in the harvest field and health in the sheepfold. When a pastoral team lacks unity, that fact cannot be hidden from the flock; and much of the teaching and modeling is negated.

I have heard it said, "I am a servant of God, not of men." While that may be so, we must also be sensitive to those who share our calling, as well as to those to whom we are ministering. The fact is that we cannot be true servants of God without being servants of men. Jesus made this truth clear to His disciples:

> "No longer do I call you servants, for a servant does not know what his master is doing; but I have called you friends, for all things that I heard from My Father I have made known to you. . . . These things I command you, that you love one another" (John 15:15, 17).

We cannot teach our people to love one another unless they see love demonstrated in our pastoral team. The most important ethical consideration we must model is the refusal to permit gossip to divide us. If we are told, "So-and-so said such-and- such about you," our response must be loving and humble. One wise pastor responded by saying, "Well, maybe something I did or said made him feel that way. You and I must go immediately and ask him."

In another situation a staff member told a pastor that several people had complained about him.

"Well, that is very serious," he responded. "Give me their names and call them to come in right away so we can hear their complaints face-to-face. Maybe we can solve the problem." The gossips in both the above situations were silenced, because the news-bearers themselves were the real malcontents.

Not one of us is perfect, and we may easily be misunderstood. An immediate, loving confrontation is the honorable manner in which to solve problems of misunderstanding. If we are serious about ministering to people, we do not want to wound or harm anyone. An *immediate* apology and plea for forgiveness are mandatory.

If leaders don't practice and demonstrate humility in these matters, how can they expect others to follow? We are to settle our differences according to Matthew 18:15-18. We are not to be judgmental, critical, or take our brother to court. Jealousy and envy in pastoral leadership are easily discerned by a congregation. On no pastoral staff or organization does everyone possess equal talents and gifts.

For example, I once knew a man who couldn't carry a tune in a bucket. In his insecurity, he made it his mission to prevent more gifted people from publicly exercising their God-given musical talents. This kind of ungodly conduct and dissension is obvious to the flock. The responsibilities of the pastoral staff call for the effective use of each person's gifts.

> Let nothing be done through selfish ambition or conceit, but in lowliness of mind let each esteem others better than himself. Let each of you look out not only for his own interests, but also for the interests of others (Philippians 2:3, 4).

If we are dedicated servants of God, each of us will make it our business to acknowledge the unique gifts of our fellow shepherds. The one who can perform the task most effectively is the one who must be permitted to do the job. In this way everyone is blessed and God's best is demonstrated. We must also take into consideration the importance of the assignment according to *ability*.

The cottage prayer meeting can be an opportunity for learning for the novice—both for himself and others. But being the guest speaker at a citywide minister's convention should be left to the veteran pulpiteer. The less-experienced minister must insist on this procedure, thus demonstrating ministerial ethics practiced for the highest glory of God and His church.

The matter of seniority in ministry must always be taken into consideration, out of respect for experience. However, if we are all sincerely attempting to present the most-gifted person for the occasion, a younger man with a more powerful preaching gift should get the call to minister, rather than one who is older and has more rank but is not so divinely gifted.

The Biblical concept expressed by Paul in the Scripture above does not refer to the best educated, most senior or best-known. Rather, it means "the most suited" or "specifically gifted" man or woman for the occasion. When we begin making assignments based on our own judgment, we run the risk of overriding God's own giftings and divine selection and stepping beyond our province of authority.

Take an example from the military. In earlier days, many tasks now performed by computers were performed by individuals trained to perform a special task. When the enemy was encountered by the Navy, the range-finding officer would discern the distance from his ship to the enemy. He communicated this information to the officer called "the gun layer," who set the elevation of the guns to correctly reach the enemy's position.

The officer in the gun turret would swing his mighty guns to the exact position, left or right, so that the enemy was lined up with his guns. The captain or gunnery officer directed the exact moment of fire, and the fire control officer fired the guns to the very second. They worked together smoothly as a team, or the battle was lost. No one ever thought of doing someone else's job. Each man knew and performed the job for which he had been trained.

Can we, as God's great military force, learn to prefer each other for the tasks for which each is best suited? True ministerial ethics require us to move as a harmonious team so that those to whom we minister may be best served in both evangelism and discipleship training.

May God help us minister in humility and unity.

CHAPTER 29

DISCIPLINED BY GRACE

*T*he world is obsessed with the performance syndrome. It is, therefore, often difficult for Christians to understand the relationship between justification by faith without works, and a life and performance that manifests a spiritual transformation as new creatures in Christ.

I have met and counseled with dozens of believers who expressed confusion about this issue. Some have told me that their newfound redemption through Christ has made them slaves to rules and religious regulations they cannot live up to.

Sometimes the judgment they had to endure from seasoned Christians had made them oversensitive to everything they were trying to do to please God. Paul wrote: "For if there is first a willing mind, it is accepted according to what one has, and not according to what he does not have" (2 Corinthians 8:12). Attitude is more important than accomplishment.

Stringent legalism is the strongest noose around Biblical liberty. Satan often uses it to neutralize our impact on others. It is liberating when a Christian discovers from the Scripture that "by grace you have been saved through faith, and that not of yourselves; it is the gift of God, not of works, lest anyone should boast" (Ephesians 2:8, 9). Paul also wrote:

> But to him who does not work but believes on Him who justifies the ungodly, his faith is accounted for righteousness (Romans 4:5).

> Therefore, my beloved, as you have always obeyed, not as in my presence only, but now much more in my absence, work out your own salvation with fear and trembling; for it is God who works in you both to will and to do for His good pleasure (Philippians 2:12, 13).

Do these powerful scriptures contradict one another? Paul clarifies the issue in 2 Corinthians 5:17: "Therefore, if anyone is in Christ, he is a new creation; old things have passed away; behold, all things have become new."

But, if I am to work out my own salvation, by

*what rules must I live, work and behave? What moti-
vation do I have to live a renewed life?* We find the
answer in Romans 8:1-4. The last part of verse 1
is not in the original Greek text, so the passage
should read:

> There is therefore now no condemnation to those who
> are in Christ Jesus. . . . For the law of the Spirit of life
> in Christ Jesus has made me free from the law of sin
> and death. For what the law could not do in that it was
> weak through the flesh, God did by sending His own
> Son in the likeness of sinful flesh, on account of sin:
> He condemned sin in the flesh, that the righteous
> requirement of the law might be fulfilled in us who do
> not walk according to the flesh but according to the
> Spirit.

By this we understand that it is impossible for
those saved by grace and born again through the
Spirit to live up to God's standards in their own
strength. Although you are a new creature in Christ,
you must *learn* to "walk in the Spirit, and you shall
not fulfill the lust of the flesh" (Galatians 5:16).
Paul further reassures us that "it is God who works
in you both to will and to do for His good pleasure"
(Philippians 2:13).

As true believers in the redemption in Jesus,
we know that as we are taught and led by the
indwelling Holy Spirit, and we can live a transformed life which becomes progressively like that
of Christ our Lord. In this light, then, how do we
reconcile the issue of being disciplined by grace,
as opposed to following a legalistic list of dos and

don'ts which have been set up by religious and sectarian leaders, and which form the foundation of a judgmental attitude toward other believers?

We must remember that *every true Christian's spiritual life is one of growth in grace and in the knowledge of God and His will.* As we learn to walk in the Spirit, we may fall short; but the apostle John writes these encouraging words:

> If we say that we have no sin, we deceive ourselves, and the truth is not in us. [But] if we confess our sins, He is faithful and just to forgive us our sins and to cleanse us from all unrighteousness. My little children, these things I write to you, so that you may not sin. And if anyone sins, we have an Advocate with the Father, Jesus Christ the righteous. And He Himself is the propitiation for our sins, and not for ours only but also for the whole world (1 John 1:8, 9; 2:1, 2).

As growing believers, we discover that some earlier thoughts and actions that troubled our consciences were not, after all, unscriptural. On the other hand, we learn that some things we did with impunity we now can no longer pursue. We also find that we learn to be sensitive about the judgment of a fellow Christian whose own conscience may be troubled by something we feel free to do. In Romans 14:10 and 1 Corinthians 8:1-13, Paul deals with this problem in depth.

When I first began to understand God's grace, it was one of the most liberating spiritual experiences I had ever had. God broke many of the chains that had bound me, and I reveled in my newfound liberty from nit-picking legalism. Regrettably, I was not always charitable toward my brethren who had not been so liberated. As I struggled to understand God's will, I began to realize that I was indeed my brother's keeper. I strove to reach other believers about what God's grace had come to mean to me. I learned that I must work gently and lovingly within the limits of their consciences in order to lead them into deeper freedom in Christ.

On a missionary journey into the jungles of Africa, I traveled with a friend. We had each packed all the food, water and other essentials we would need. I had purchased an expensive can of salt-cured bacon and looked forward to frying it over an open fire in the bush. When I opened it I saw that my friend was deeply concerned. "You are not going to eat that pork, are you?" he asked.

He told me that neither he nor his parents had ever eaten pork because it was condemned in the Old Testament. At first I was inwardly annoyed. But before I defended my freedom, I remembered Paul's admonition: "Therefore, if food makes my brother stumble, I will never again eat meat, lest I make my brother stumble" (1 Corinthians 8:13). I suddenly realized that my Christian brother's conscience saw the eating of that bacon as uncharitable on my part. Consequently, the hyenas found an open can of bacon at our abandoned campsite!

Later, I found the opportunity to speak gently to him about the legalism that bound him. I reminded him that God had good reason to condemn the camp-scavenging swine that plagued Israel during their journey through the desert. However, I commented, the pork we consume today comes from hogs that have been carefully fed. They present no health hazard for us.

I mentioned that Paul warned Timothy that some teachers would forbid people from eating certain foods which God had created to be received with thanksgiving: "For everything God created is good, and nothing is to be rejected if it is received with thanksgiving, because it is consecrated by the word of God and prayer" (1 Timothy 4:4, 5, *NIV*). A few days later I rejoiced inwardly when my friend said to me, "You know, I was wrong when I encouraged you to throw away that good bacon."

I urge each of you to realize that we have been called to liberty (Galatians 5:13), but we must not use that liberty to walk roughshod over a weaker brother's conscience. Those who are disciplined by grace are loving, patient and nonjudgmental.

CHAPTER 30

ENTERTAINMENT IN THE SANCTUARY

*A*n inexplicable phenomenon is taking place in the contemporary Christian assembly. Much is being said and written about "worship leaders" or the "worship team" that takes part in the service. Yet, more often than not, it seems it is not genuine worship that is sought as much as it is a crowd-pleasing emotional response.

In the Old Testament, priests led the worship with the participation of musicians and vocalists. Since the Cross, however, it has been primarily the task of the pastor to set the tone of worship. He is assisted by the choir director or a special worship leader who leads the congregation in songs of praise and exaltation. In many cases no real effort is put forth to emphasize the sense of the presence of God. Excitement and physical abandon at a fever pitch supposedly lead us to believe that this kind of activity in God's house is the way to come into close communion with Him.

Crowds now come to church for no other reason than to find a mental escape into a quasi-mysticism that enables them to momentarily forget their troubles. Some leaders encourage the belief that the Holy Spirit is Himself engineering this mindless journey into a spiritual never-never land. The redeeming Christ never appears as the central figure in this tryst with unreality, but the one involved "feels better" because he experiences a rhapsodic emotional dimension. The Word of God is minimized and, in some cases, totally ignored.

I have met worship leaders who knew little or nothing about true worship. A devout music minister in a large church took his choir to a spiritual retreat. He secured the services of a gifted evangelist and also invited a "dynamic worship leader." The powerful speaker challenged and deeply moved the choir members who came forward to the altar for personal heart-searching and prayer. One evening the worship leader asked the choir director why choir members were praying and crying around the altar. He didn't have a clue. He could lead them in a rousing "Jericho March" around the meeting hall, but he had no idea how to lead them to the throne of God!

More can be said about some of the music appearing in modern worship services. A genuine student of God's Word recognizes that the individuals who wrote both the lyrics and melodies of some of the songs demonstrated a dearth of knowledge of Scriptures. They sought to create emotions by repetition. There is nothing wrong with shouting, rejoicing and dancing "in the Spirit" as long as it truly *is* in the Spirit and becomes a celebration of God's holy presence.

The priests of the Old Testament danced before God as they held high the ancient Torah. So did King David! I have been a charismatic Christian for 65 years and have participated in true worship services where there was such a sense of the divine presence that we felt the Lord Jesus Christ himself was standing among us in the presence of His Father.

I have also been a keen observer at pagan festivals where Satan-worshipers, followers of witchcraft, and African witch doctors led a heathen crowd in an orgy of emotional and physical abandonment that caused them to strip off their clothing, cut themselves with stones and pieces of glass, dash through fire, and dance in wild mimicry of the sex act. When they finally collapsed in exhaustion, they raved to one another about what a wonderful experience it had been. Those pagan leaders achieved a "crowd-pleasing emotional response," but the experience was evil, debasing and horrifying because of the lifestyle it encouraged among the so-called worshipers.

Ways to influence an audience have been the subject of research and study for a long time. Some eloquent speakers have literally led their people into the very presence of God. Others have created mob violence by their public addresses. Adolf Hitler was a master at stirring up the youth of Germany. I have seen skillful pulpiteers move a crowd to empty their pockets for a cause that did not merit such generosity. Simply moving an audience to tears, to ecstasy or to sacrificial giving must never be our objective. If it is, our listeners will eventually discern that our motives are self-centered.

The minister's sole motive in moving an audience must be to encourage people to take appropriate action. In God's house, every experience must challenge people to a personal relationship with God through Jesus Christ. An exhilarating atmosphere that simply causes them to "feel good" is nothing but religious and social chaff.

Every evangelist, pastor or worship leader must ask himself what he wants to inspire his listeners to do. If he only wants to make them laugh, he is no more than an ecclesiastical comedian. If he wants to impress them with his mastery of the language, he is merely a skillful orator. If he wants to get his hands into their pockets, he is an impostor and a thief. However, if his heart's desire is to lead them to Christ and turn from their wicked ways, he qualifies as a true servant of God.

I have spoken to a number of disappointed worshipers. Their greatest complaint has been that while the church service was entertaining, provided a warm social gathering and in some cases was intellectually stimulating, they did not sense the presence of God. Although the leaders themselves seemed to feel they had accomplished the will of God in the service, there was no hint that the presence of God was important.

There is a difference between the person who says he enjoyed a pleasant service and one who says that he sensed the presence of God and the Holy Spirit. If people come to church to socialize and meet friends, where are they supposed to go to meet God? We must not get caught up in this error. We go to God's house first to meet *Him*. Only then can we greet our brothers and sisters in the warmth and love of Christian fellowship.

> There will be a time when they will not bear with healthy teaching, but according to their own burning lusts they will heap up to themselves teachers that tickle their ears (2 Timothy 4:3, original Greek text).

Some render the last phrase, "teachers who like to have their ears tickled!" When church members are entranced with our pastoral eloquence or musical talent to the point of adulation, we should be shocked into watchfulness. Do we want parishioners to say, "Wasn't the pastor marvelous this week?" Or, "I felt the presence of Jesus in a marvelous way"? Certainly our leadership should be exciting and refreshing, but only because of the God-given skills we demonstrate in leading people into the presence of the King.

An American businessman visited England at the peak of Charles Spurgeon's ministry. His host invited him to attend church with him, and in the morning they visited the Englishman's home congregation. The sermon was an oratorical masterpiece, and the businessman was impressed with the skillful presentation. That evening they heard Spurgeon speak under great anointing.

Afterward, the Englishman asked, "Well, what did you think of the preacher you heard this morning?" The American replied, "He is a fabulous orator!" "But what did you think of Pastor Spurgeon?" asked the host.

"Oh," replied his guest, "Isn't Jesus wonderful!" In the morning service the speaker's skills had been exalted. In Spurgeon's sermon, Christ was lifted up.

This is the secret of every Christ-centered preacher's success. As pastors, who are we lifting up?

CHAPTER 31

SPIRITUAL UNITY: A TIMELY AWAKENING

*I*n more than 60 years of preaching the gospel, I have had the privilege of working with many men and women of God—a few of them notable, like Dr. Billy Graham, Dr. Jack Hayford and Dr. Paul L. Walker. Many others were unknown except locally, where they spent years of service for Christ. Some were closely associated with one denomination or another. Others were not members of any particular fellowship.

I have ministered in every continent, except South America, with people of varied ethnic groups. With them I have been deeply moved by the glory and majesty of the body of Christ. There were many forms of worship, so many languages and such a variation of doctrinal reflections. Yet, this heterogeneous multitude of saints, in total spiritual unity, gazed enraptured into the face of Jesus Christ, the Son of God. This marvelous family must always observe these Biblical principles of fellowship:

- The basic truths of the Holy Scriptures must be accepted and declared.

- Fellow worshipers must observe and accept the absolute lordship of Jesus Christ.

All else is secondary and can be charitably worked out. Memory takes me back to worship experiences ranging from the rhythmic cadences in an African jungle to the thundering crescendo of a 300-voice choir singing the finale of Handel's *Messiah*. What contrasts I have witnessed and experienced—from the dust and heat of a woven thorn *boma* to the air-conditioned comfort of a modern Christian cathedral; from the most primitive to the most sophisticated. In every case, Christ was the unquestioned object of worship.

But one thing always troubled me—the schisms, rivalries and bigotry that sometimes separate this marvelous body of Christians. I've seen believers agree on basic tenets of the Christian faith, yet separate from each other by such human traits as snobbish intolerance and ethnic bigotry. We are known by our fruits. It is not by any of the "things" we sometimes use to gain acceptance with one another.

Trivial doctrinal differences and denominationalism produce unimaginable divisions in the body of Christ. I am not against either denominationalism or nondenominationalism. I spent my ministry in a well-known denomination simply because I felt led of the Lord to do so. However, I have met many of God's servants who felt just as definitely led to serve God outside of denominational associations.

I have discovered that the fundamental Biblical criterion of one's Christian commitment rests on spiritual relationship with the Lord Jesus Christ, not on human associations. The bottom line in Christian religious assessment is this: *Is Christ being proclaimed as Lord and Savior to a lost and sinful world?* He said that if He was lifted up He would draw all men unto Himself. Are we lifting Him up? Recent polls revealed that more than 50 percent of all Christians preferred spiritual association with a fellowship controlled and operated locally rather than from a geographic center far from the place of worship.

This means that more and more congregations with no denominational affiliation are springing up. Their pastors often have great trouble gaining licensed or ordained status that is recognized by either local, state or national governments. In spite of these difficulties, they are growing as rapidly and having as great an impact for Christ as those fellowships that are denominationally aligned. When ministering in churches not affiliated with a denomination, I have sensed as great a move of the Holy Spirit as I felt in the great 10,000-plus membership of the church where I served in a denomination.

One of our problems as Christians is that we often live in a self-created vacuum, supported and encouraged by our aloofness and religious pride. Consequently, we don't know what is happening to the body of Christ around the world. We seem unaware that the 20th century saw more Christian martyrs than all of the 19 preceding centuries combined!

A godless world does not recognize our varied divisions and doctrinal concepts. Persecutors hate all Christians without distinction. Consequently, there are countries in which all Christians are suffering severe persecution and, very often, martyrdom. In those areas we have discovered that fellowship and unity are 100 percent stronger than in places where persecution is almost unheard of.

Here is a galling question: *Why is it that we as Christians seem to have to wait until persecution strikes to discover our mutual faith and spiritual unity?* What about our doctrinal differences? Do we really mean "doctrinal differences"? Are we sure that we are not actually speaking of different forms of worship or liturgy? If we agree that the basic principle is the lordship of Jesus Christ, then we must allow each other the freedom to worship and interpret God's Word in whatever way we choose.

We must, in turn, express and model our own unique interpretation of Christianity as brethren in Christ. The fierce hatred some factions of Christianity have raised against others who profess the same faith is nothing less than satanic in its devastating division of the brethren. We are the only world religion that has fractionalized itself into hundreds of varied groupings. Judaism deals with two or three. Islam is about the same. Most other non-Christian faiths are not so divided or at odds with one another.

When we stand in the presence of Jesus, the fierce insistence that our interpretation of His words and the Christian faith is the only Biblical one that will be seen as sectarian arrogance. This unfortunate tendency has torn the body of Christ into a thousand groups who do not fellowship with each other. Our disunity is a disgrace created by professed believers in Christ and is due to distrust and judgmental attitudes toward others. We make the prayer of our Lord a laughing matter in the eyes of a "religious" but non-Christian world (see John 17:11, 21, 22).

I emphasize the overwhelming need to seek *compassionately* the similarities between our own view of doctrinal and practical priorities, and the view of others on the same matters. Let us cease our small-minded scrutiny of areas of disagreement. Look honestly and seriously for those facts of faith on which we do agree. You will find, as I have, that there is far more unanimity than conflict in our mutual concepts of what is important in presenting the gospel to a lost society.

Certainly there are differences.But only those which God's Word identifies as heresies should claim our attention. Even then we should be more concerned with loving correction than with judgmental comments or actions. Years ago I set up a criteria for basic fellowship with other Christians who did not see eye-to-eye with me.

I decided that if another person accepted the fatherhood of God as Creator, the sonship and deity of Christ, His virgin birth, His fundamental teachings, His miracles while here on earth, His vicarious substitutionary death, His bodily resurrection, and His second coming, that person was my brother or sister. Denominational affiliation is not all that important.

I rejoice in the fact that I have been asked to serve on ministerial fellowships in denominational and nondenominational settings. I always encourage trans-cultural and transdenominational fellowships within the body of Christ until He returns.

CHAPTER 32

THE POVERTY OF A NOVELTY RELIGION

*T*he best English dictionaries define the word *religion*: "Recognition on the part of man of a controlling, superhuman power entitled to obedience, reverence and worship; the spiritual attitude of those recognizing such a controlling power; also the manifestation of such feeling and recognition in conduct of life."

From the difficult days of the early church until recently, attendance at the house of God brought certain expectations that are not always evident in our time. Worshipers and visitors alike seldom expected an experience of pure unchallenged tranquility and undisturbed peace. Instead, they knew they would be aroused to face the sin question in their own lives and consciences. "They were cut to the heart, and said to Peter and the rest of the apostles, 'Men and brethren, what shall we do?'"(Acts 2:37).

From Peter's time until now, we have been told that we need to get right with God. Paul said that if Christian believers preached or publicly prophesied, unbelievers and unlearned people who were present among them would be convicted of their sins and would fall down on their faces and worship God, realizing that God was present in their midst (1 Corinthians 14:24, 25). The Holy Spirit reveals the sinfulness of humanity to the sinner and leads him to repentance. That has always been the effect of the work of the Spirit in our hearts, whether we have accepted Christ or not.

Years ago an evangelist delivered a powerful message on "The Sin That Doth So Easily Beset Us." A friend whom I had known for years as a devout Christian tugged on my sleeve and said, "Please come to the altar with me. God has convicted me of sin that I have permitted to slip into my life. I need to confess it and be forgiven in the sight of my Lord." I still don't know what the sin was, but his prayer was in earnest. He arose from his knees justified.

According to some contemporary preaching, God is no longer concerned about sin. Sinful people are not told to repent and turn away from disobedience and rebellion. Attendance at God's house brings no challenge to forsake sin and godless living. Instead, church attendance has become a novelty experience in many cases, much like going to a circus. In fact, some senior pastors are encouraging their staffs to do their utmost to make people feel comfortable and enjoy the show. Nothing is said about a sinful lifestyle. To them, God has become simply a God of benevolence, peace and love.

Christians must always keep in mind that while Christianity exemplifies the love of God for the lost and the sinful, it is intolerant toward sin. It always calls sin "SIN" and tells of *one* way to eternal life—the way of the Cross through the redemptive work of Christ (see John 14:6). On the other hand, God is a gracious and forgiving Father who bids us come openly and without fear to Him.

> Seeing then that we have a great High Priest who has passed through the heavens, Jesus the Son of God, let us hold fast our confession. For we do not have a High Priest who cannot sympathize with our weaknesses, but was in all points tempted as we are, yet without sin. Let us therefore come boldly to the throne of grace, that we may obtain mercy and find grace to help in time of need (Hebrews 4:14-16).

During the earlier decades of this century, a well-known agnostic expressed the opinion that the greatest creation of the human mind was a thoroughly benevolent god. Dr. B.B. Warfield, a noted Christian scholar, responded by saying that the uninspired mind of unregenerate man would never create for itself a god of holiness, righteousness, mercy and justice. That kind of god would bring sinful men either under judgment or spiritual and moral transformation. Neither could be tolerated in the minds of unregenerate but religious hedonists.

Doctor Warfield's knowledge of both fallen and redeemed humanity told him that no unregenerate mind would invent a deity that would make spiritual, moral and ethical demands on its creatures. The God of the Bible is not such a deity. He makes moral, ethical and spiritual demands of those who are His children.

A believer's religious concepts and behavior are a microcosm of his fundamental concept of God. If he sees God as sovereign, just and righteous—and acknowledges Him with holy awe and reverence—his lifestyle and worship will reflect these views. Further, as a born-again child of God he will be deeply moved by the love of God that was manifested in the life and ministry of Jesus Christ. He will be deeply moved by the sovereign justice of God manifested in the substitutionary death of Christ on his behalf.

The price paid for our wonderful salvation and new standing before God is not to be taken lightly. It involved the self-abnegation of the co-Creator of the universe who made Himself a servant to sinners like us, and who endured the ignominy and agony of the cross to redeem us from our sins.

I do not suggest that we enter God's house with abject fear or long-faced, feigned piety. God's Word instructs us to enter His courts with praise and thanksgiving. Our entrance into His presence should create joy unspeakable and a peace that passes understanding.

On the other hand, there are those like the young man who came into my office for counseling some years ago. He recounted a number of lifestyle "experiments" he had tried, some of them both morally and ethically borderline in execution. Without missing a breath he continued, "I have done all these things for 'kicks,' now I've come to try out this Christianity thing."

Even God's people sometimes get caught up in religious sensationalism. I have attended worship services where the musical renditions were performed with perfection, and the preaching was homiletically excellent, entertaining and humorous.

Afterward it occurred to me that I had not sensed the presence of God or the deeper concepts of faith during the entire service. The level of human sociality was exciting and the fluctuating psyches of many were psychologically lulled into a temporary sense of euphoria. The entire program was a masterpiece of both rhythm and organization, but I doubt that God would call it a worship service.

I have attended many marvelous theatrical performances with professional actors, and I got just what I went for—the exciting novelty of wholesome entertainment. I sometimes wonder if I would have discerned any essential difference between the "performance" in the theater and that in the sanctuary of God, had I not been a Christian. As ministers *of* God *to* people, we are honor-bound to seriously examine our own "performance."

The father in a poverty-ridden family died, leaving behind his wife and young son. The widowed mother became desperately ill and a friend took a Christian doctor to see her. After examining her he said to his friend in an adjoining room, "If someone does not find God for this woman, she will not live long." He didn't realize that her 6-year-old son had heard his remark.

On Sunday morning an usher in a nearby church saw the poorly clad boy enter the sanctuary. He asked if he could help him. The boy said, "Is God here?" When the usher took the child to the pastor, he asked again, "Is God here?" The pastor took the child by the hand and stood him beside the pulpit. He explained the situation to the congregation, then asked, "What do you think? Is God here?"

He was indeed! The congregation responded in the spirit of Christ and provided the medical attention the woman needed and financial assistance as well. The church became an ongoing spiritual and social refuge for the widow and her son.

Does God go to your church?

CHAPTER 33

THE BIBLICAL DEMAND FOR PASTORAL CONSTANCY

n fatherly instruction to his pastor-protégé, Timothy, Paul gave some comprehensive instruction in 2 Timothy 4:2: "Preach the word of God. Be persistent, whether the time is favorable or not. Patiently correct, rebuke, and encourage your people with good teaching."

The literal translation of the original Greek text states, "Proclaim the Word; be attentive seasonably, unseasonably; reprove, admonish, exhort, with all long-suffering and teaching." These instructions to his young friend describe the responsibilities and challenges of pastoral ministry. No task on earth is more difficult or stressful. Some have the idea that pastoral life is easy, with few serious responsibilities or burdens. Nothing could be further from the truth. It is a 24-hour-a-day assignment. It is providing effective comfort and sympathy, while conducting funerals for those both in and out of the congregation. It is counseling dysfunctional families, the emotionally distressed and those in financial difficulty. These and other human traumas comprise the active pastor's daily routine.

The pastor must also be prepared to officiate at weddings, graduations and church conferences. Often he sits with his church council as they discuss the management and direction of the local church. He must learn to lead and shepherd people, not all of whom are meek and sheep-like in their reactions to majority decisions of the church council or board of directors.

The pastor must be a peacemaker, a teacher, a gifted and inspiring speaker, one who encourages, and one who can lead a congregation in worship. His devotion to God, his prayer life and his love for God's Word are absolute essentials for success in the pulpit and counseling office. Lest we forget, he must also be a lover of people.

I recall chatting with a young pas toral assistant. When I asked him how he liked his work, he responded, "Oh, it would not be bad at all if it were not for the people. Sometimes I find it hard to put up with their childish behaviors." I told him what

I have said before: If a pastor cannot weep with those who weep, he will never have the luxury of rejoicing with those who rejoice. This speaks of what must be inside the head and heart of those who feel led of God to take up the pastoral task. Look at Paul's instructions.

1. The pastor must be a preacher. He must be one who proclaims God's Word. I have discussed this subject in depth in the chapter "Preach the Word." But it is obviously the most essential point of a pastor's work and cannot be too strongly emphasized again. I remind you that this calls for the ability of the preacher to correctly interpret the Holy Scriptures as he prepares his message.

This requires good basic training in methods of study. It calls for preaching genuine truth from the Bible. Most of all, it requires time for study in order to interpret God's Word for his people. Living in a constantly changing society, the pastor often studies far into the night.

Paul instructed Timothy to "study to shew thyself approved unto God, a workman that needeth not to be ashamed, rightly dividing the word of truth" (2 Timothy 2:15, KJV). While it is true that a pastor must constantly visit his people, he must make the time to get alone with God, the Bible and his own soul as he prepares his sermons.

2. The pastor must be diligent. It is imperative

for the pastor to fulfill his tasks, whether he feels like it or not. There is no Biblical excuse for lethargy or lazy commitment to the needs of the people. As demands on his time increased, Martin Luther declared, "I have become so busy that I have had to take an extra hour for prayer every day if I am to finish my daily tasks." Sometimes those midnight hours, though "out of season," are essential if the pastor is to fully accomplish his God-given assignment.

3. The pastor must reprove. This means "to correct." The task requires courage, wisdom, accurate knowledge, and enough love for the person in error to speak to him lovingly and clearly. The ancient shepherd carried a rod with a hook on the end, with which he would catch the erring sheep, and gently and skillfully draw it back from the precipice and into the fold. Error must never be met by criticism until it is lovingly defined by the shepherd. To ostracize the erring is never the solution in correcting error.

Years ago I was asked by a gentle and loving pastor to be present at a very difficult session in his church. One of the families in his congregation had misled another and taught a seriously false doctrine. The pastor had tried to persuade the erring family to recant, but they adamantly refused. Finally, with tears streaming down his face he expressed brokenheartedly that he would be forced to disfellowship that family. Suddenly, the offending father stood weeping, and apologized for the confusion he and his family had caused. He pled for the pastor and church to forgive and restore them. The pastor, his wife and elders lovingly took that family in their arms and forgave them.

4. The pastor must rebuke. This term is best defined "to admonish"; it has the flavor of loving correction. A dictionary meaning is "to give friendly, earnest advice or encouragement." Outside the ancient walls of Jerusalem, an Arab shepherd told me that the difference between a butcher and a shepherd is that a butcher *drives* his sheep, but a shepherd *leads* them! David said, "He restores my soul; He leads me in the paths of righteousness for His name's sake" (Psalm 23:3).

5. The pastor must exhort. This means "to encourage." He must constantly reassure his people in order to fill them with courage and strength for the challenges of daily living. He must walk in their shoes. The Scriptural standard for a pastor is the same as that of his flock; God's Word does not teach a double standard.

I can recall days of discouragement when words of appreciation and support from my people gave me the incentive and faith to persevere.

I had the privilege of closing my primary Christian ministry under the leadership of a man who is one of God's "professional encouragers." He quoted many scriptures in his sermons, and his favorite was: "I can do all things through Christ who strengthens me" (Philippians 4:13).

Paul's final phrase in 2 Timothy 4:2 has to do with patience. This powerful text tells us to do all of the above-mentioned things with "long-suffering and teaching." *Long-suffering* means "great patience." It speaks of both attitude and activity.

Teaching, whether part of a sermon or in the pastor's Bible class, is the most important assignment God has given His pastoral servants. Great truths must be repeated patiently until they become part of what Christians know as "the faith." Jesus was called "Teacher" more than He was called "Preacher" in the New Testament.

Let me encourage you, my pastor friend, to persevere under the unusual stress of pastoral ministry. Like Luther, spend enough time in prayer to get your work done.

CHAPTER 34

THE FINAL WORD: THE GRACE OF GOD

*A*t the end of this work, I wish to add a few Biblically instructive words on the subject of the grace of God. In spite of critics, Christianity has survived because it transforms the way people think, live and behave. The most wicked human beings have been transformed into happy, productive persons with unsullied records of spotless integrity.

There have been unscrupulous hypocrites who claimed to be Christians but were not. Every religion and philosophy has its pretenders. History has proven that even communism developed its own crop of political frauds.

The fact is that every true Christian is in an endless process of spiritual growth. Lest we become wearied in this lifelong process, we should be encouraged by the Biblical realities of God's grace.

1. Our redemption and subsequent transformation are an act of God that enables us to grow "In Christ."

> That in the ages to come He might show the exceeding riches of His grace in His kindness toward us in Christ Jesus. For by grace you have been saved through faith, and that not of yourselves; it is the gift of God, not of works, lest anyone should boast (Ephesians 2:7-9).

We are living manifestations of the divine transformation of God's salvation. Growth in Christ includes a growing triumph over sin. Further, we have the assurance of God's help throughout our lives.

2. We are in the continual safekeeping of God.
Our growth in Him and in real holiness is assured because we have continual access to His grace: "Through whom also we have access by faith into this grace in which we stand, and rejoice in hope of the glory of God" (Romans 5:2).

3. We are the servants of God, and His Spirit gives us the grace and the power to perform His service.
Jesus said, "As You sent Me into the world, I also have sent them into the world"

(John 17:18). Paul's comment adds the assurance, "But to each one of us grace was given according to the measure of Christ's gift" (Ephesians 4:7). We are not expected to do it alone; when we try we fail.

4. We can count on the Holy Spirit's leadership and continual instruction. His gracious guidance is assured. Paul wrote:

> For the grace of God that brings salvation has appeared to all men, teaching us that, denying ungodliness and worldly lusts, we should live soberly, righteously, and godly in the present age (Titus 2:11, 12).

This assures us, as Christians, of the Holy Spirit's inner teaching and guidance in our thought life. Thinking sober, righteous and godly thoughts is actually *learning to think with God.* As we recognize and experience the reality of the old fleshly nature, as opposed to our "new creature" nature, we begin to experience deliverance from the power of sin that had formerly controlled us. We can now differentiate between the two.

As Christians, every motivation or inclination that comes into focus is from our fleshly minds or from our spiritually renewed minds. Paul described the activities of the old mind prior to regeneration:

> And you He made alive, who were dead in trespasses and sins, in which you once walked according to the course of this world, according to the prince of the

power of the air, the spirit who now works in the sons of disobedience, among whom also we all once conducted ourselves in the lusts of our flesh, fulfilling the desires of the flesh and of the mind, and were by nature children of wrath, just as the others (Ephesians 2:1-3).

In another epistle, Paul identified regenerative spiritual transformation as being the "transformation of our mind":

I beseech you therefore, brethren, by the mercies of God, that you present your bodies a living sacrifice, holy, acceptable to God, which is your reasonable service. And do not be conformed to this world, but be transformed by the renewing of your mind, that you may prove what is that good and acceptable and perfect will of God (Romans 12:1, 2).

In Romans 7:25, the apostle Paul identifies *the method* of discerning the true nature of the inclinations of our mind: "I thank God—through Jesus Christ our Lord!" Our old, fleshly mind, with all its evil creativity, can only serve the law or rulership of sin. Only the spiritually renewed mind can serve the law or lordship of Jesus Christ.

Verse 25 concludes: "So then, with the mind I myself serve the law of God, but with the flesh the law of sin." Paul further declares:

But the natural man does not receive the things of the Spirit of God, for they are foolishness to him; nor can he know them, because they are spiritually discerned. But he who is spiritual judges all things, yet he himself is rightly judged by no one. For "who has known the mind of the Lord that he may instruct

Him? But we have the mind of Christ (1 Corinthians 2:14-16).

The New Testament clearly teaches that what we call "walking in the Spirit" involves a continual spiritual and mental process of learning to think with the leading of the Holy Spirit. If we are trying to walk with God, we must also learn to *think* with Him.

The Holy Spirit is our instructor in this lifelong learning process. It is the result of *positive, daily, decisive* mental and spiritual discipline. We will never achieve holiness through mental laziness. We must be continually vigilant, "casting down arguments and every high thing that exalts itself against the knowledge of God, bringing every thought into captivity to the obedience of Christ" (2 Corinthians 10:5).

For one who is truly searching, this is, indeed, the final word in moving toward personal discovery of a daily triumph over sin. Paul expressed it powerfully in Galatians 2:20:

> I am crucified with Christ: nevertheless I live; yet not I, but Christ liveth in me: and the life which I now live in the flesh I live by the faith of the Son of God, who loved me, and gave himself for me (KJV).

Being an effective, victorious Christian means growing spiritually until Jesus Christ lives in and through every thought, word, deed and action. May each of us walk so close to our Lord that others will see Him living in us and through us. This is true holiness!